HUNSTRETE
Truth and Legend
The Story of a Country Estate

Susan Elizabeth Caola

September 2003

Illustrated by Rosemary Murphy

This book is dedicated to my Mum, who shares my interest in local history, and my Dad, who would have been so proud, had he lived to see it completed.

Published by Susan Elizabeth Caola

Printed by Direct Offset, 27c High Street, Glastonbury, Somerset BA6 9DR

ISBN No: 0-9546239-0-8

Contents

Introduction

This book is the culmination of more than four years research into the history of the Hunstrete Estate. The task is not finished, as I have by no means completed an in depth assessment of all the available evidence. The sheer volume of material would render this a lifetime's work. I have, however, examined in some detail all the material that I consider both relevant and accessible. In doing so I have been able to confirm some theories and disprove others.

Much that has been written in the past about Hunstrete, has been based on secondary rather than primary evidence, leading to the continued perpetration of many inaccuracies. Where the origin of material is doubtful, I have indicated so in the text.

The history of Hunstrete has proved both fascinating, and at times frustrating where there have been incomplete records. It is an intriguing tale, interwoven with fact and fabrication and spanning many centuries. It is a story of privilege and poverty, lordship and servitude, integrity and dishonesty, and much more.

When I started I had no idea that it would become all encompassing and that I would end up on a journey following leads abroad as well as in this country. I am grateful to the many people I have met along the way who have shared their knowledge and experiences with me. I have gained a great deal of pleasure from this and hope that I have compiled as true a record of the Hunstrete Estate as is possible.

I have checked and rechecked all material but apologise for any errors that may occur. I should be grateful for any further information that anyone can provide and I may be contacted through Hunstrete House Hotel.

Susan Elizabeth Caola September 2003

Derivation of the Name Hunstrete

The hamlet of Hunstrete has down through the ages been known as: Houndesterte, Houndstreet, Hounstreet, Hounstrete, Hownstreat, Hundestert, Hundesterte, Hundestret, Hunstert, Hunstreet and Hunstreete.

Throughout the book I have used the most recent spelling of Hunstrete, except where it is taken from documentation. In such instances I have quoted verbatim.

The meaning of the name has given rise to much conjecture and no definitive answer has been found. The various suggestions, together with their sources, are given below so that the reader may make up their own mind. In the definitions below (OE) is Old or Saxon English and (ON) Old Norse.

> From the personal name HUND (OE) and STEORT (OE) meaning a projecting piece of land or the end of a piece of land.

This occurs in other Anglo Saxon charter place names.

> From the personal name HUNDR (ON) and TUN (OE) meaning a fence or enclosure around a piece of land.

As Hunstrete was known to have had a game enclosure in Anglo Saxon times, this would seem logical.

> From the word HUND (OE) as in 'hound' meaning a place where dogs were kept. Combined with either STEORT (OE) or TUN (OE).

This is difficult to distinguish from the personal names quoted above.

> From the word HUN (OE) meaning the main road of the hundred, an old unit of administration, and STRAET (OE) a Roman or paved road.

As Hunstrete lies only five miles west of Bath, on the route from the lead mines of the Mendips, whose output was used in the construction of the Roman Baths, this also merits consideration.

There may indeed be other theories as to how Hunstrete acquired its name but I have yet to discover these.

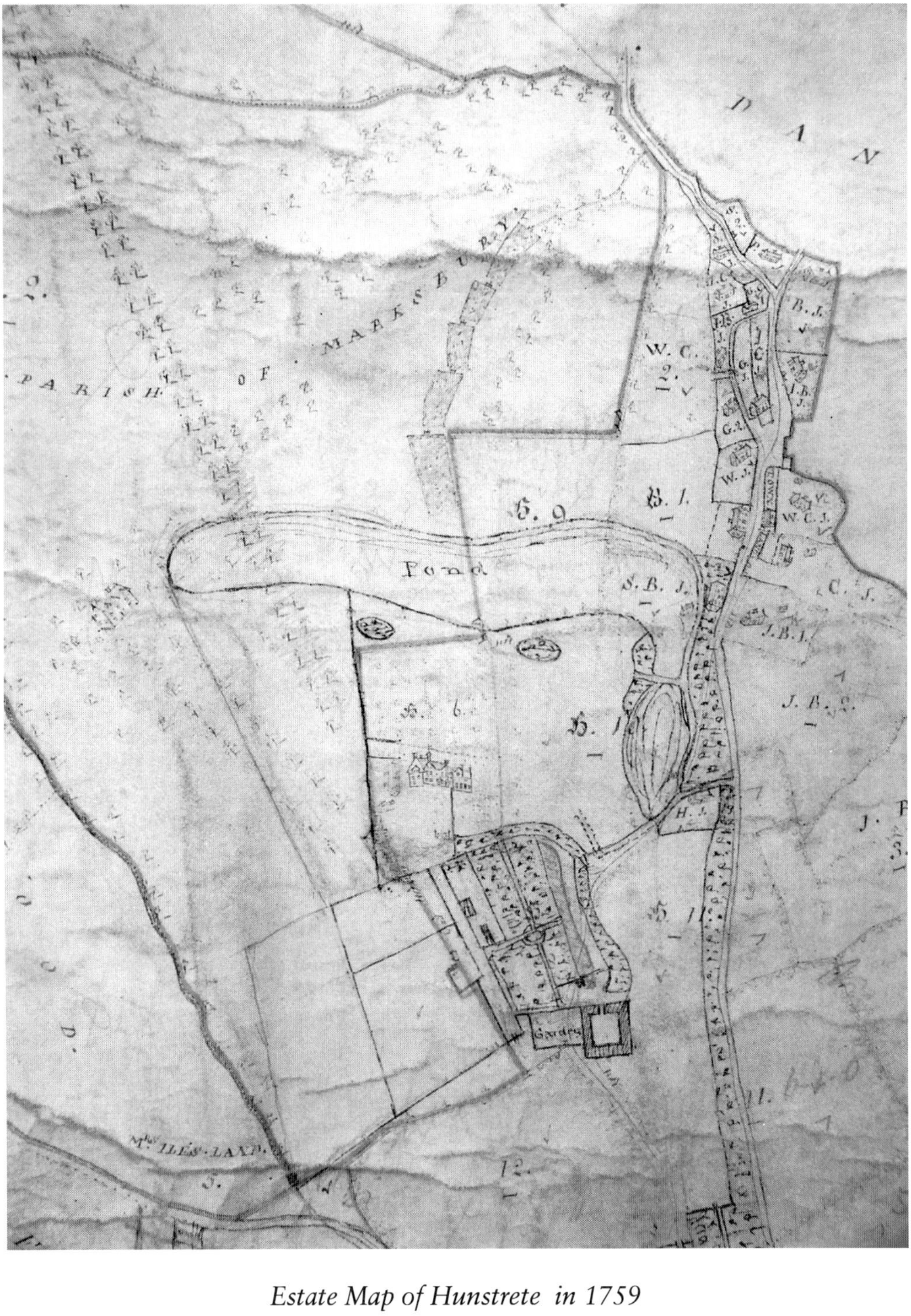

Estate Map of Hunstrete in 1759

Manorial Map of Hunstrete in 1806

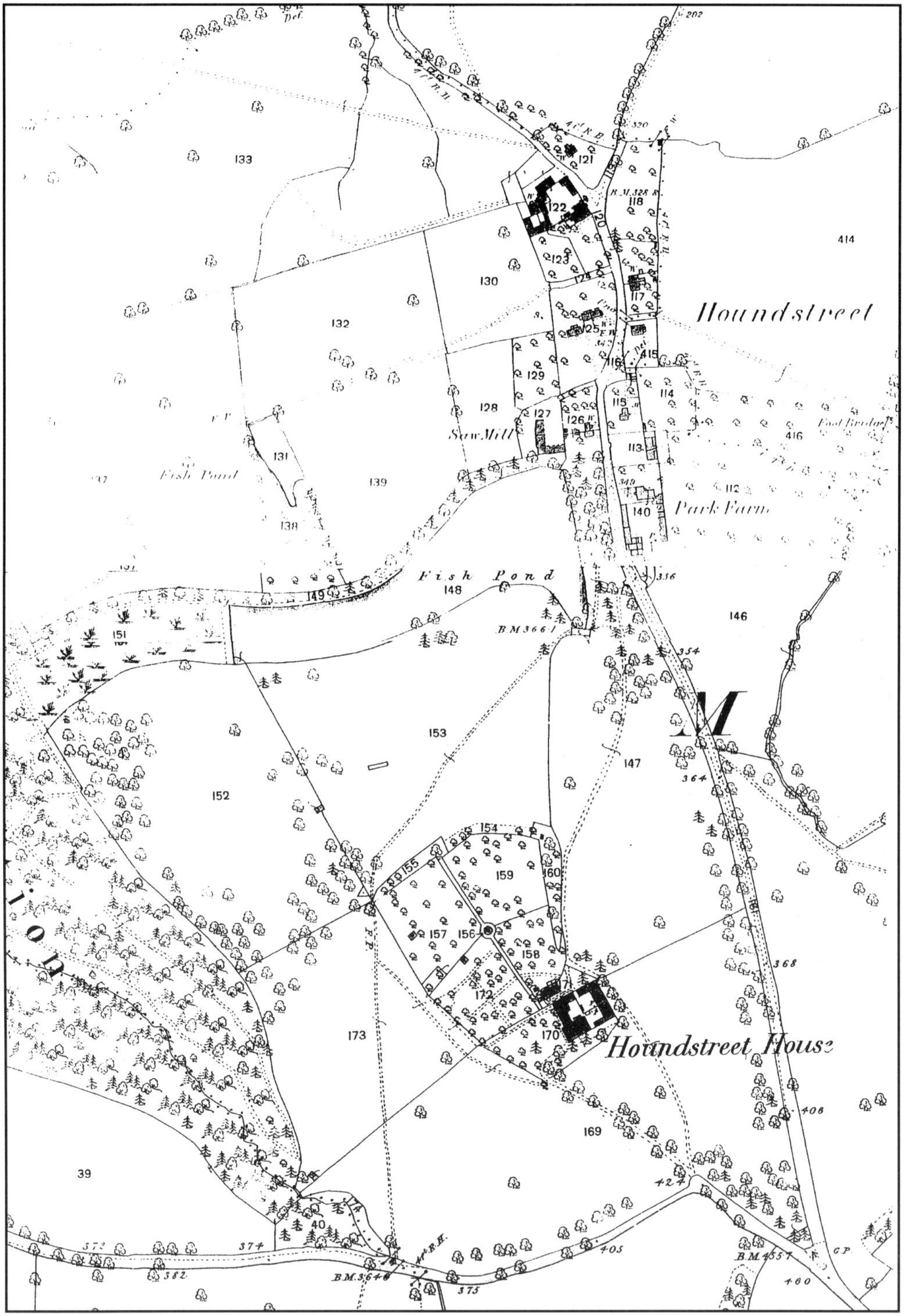

Ordnance Survey map of Hunstreet, 1882

Early Times

The hamlet of Hunstrete, in the parish of Marksbury, with its stone cottages and grand house, sits amid rolling green hills some five miles west of Bath. The area with its natural springs, extensive woodland and fertile soil was ideal for settlement and has been inhabited since the earliest times. A flint axe head, found in Common Wood, suggests that our Stone Age ancestors may well have lived here. Similarly the existence of an Iron Age fort on Stantonbury Hill, about a mile or so to the north east of Hunstrete, is also indicative of early occupation.

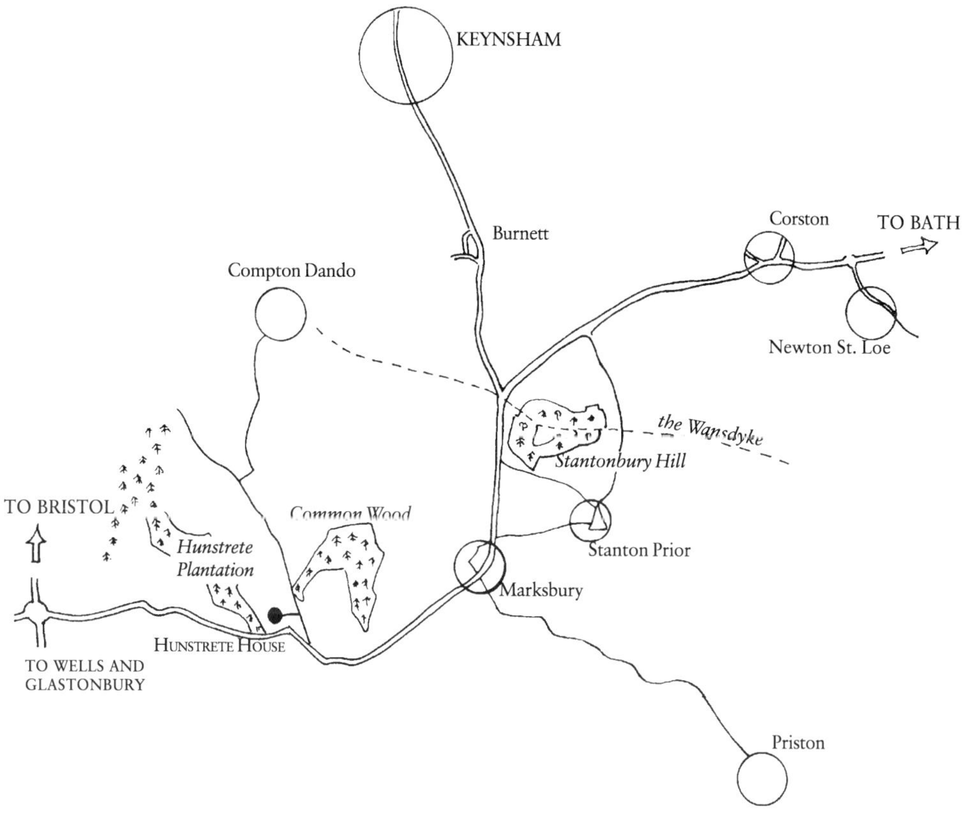

The Roman Period

By Roman times the area, with its proximity to Aquae Sulis, or Bath as it is now known, was indeed settled. Several coins from the period have been found at Hunstrete. These are almost certainly from the reign of the Emperor Carausius AD286 - 293. Surrounding villages have all yielded Roman artefacts. The most noteworthy of these are as follows:

The remains of a refuse pit from the period in Harris's quarry at Marksbury, revealed in 1937, which contained animal bones, antlers and pottery.

Traces of a Roman villa, discovered at Burnett in 1830, including a tessellated pavement and several small rooms.

A stone coffin found in 1890, in a nearby field, containing a woman's skeleton, which may or may not be linked to the building.

Evidence of a Romano British settlement in Compton Dando, uncovered in the 1980's, the site of which has yielded pottery, coins, a loom weight and several hundred broken clay moulds used in the manufacture of brooches.

With other villas discovered at Newton St Loe and also at Somerdale and Durley Hill in Keynsham, it may well be that Hunstrete was part of a thriving community.

Broken clay moulds used in the manufacture of Roman brooches

The Saxon Period

With the departure of the Romans from Britain and the subsequent decline of Aquae Sulis, it is unclear as to how many of these settlements were abandoned. However, occupation of the Hunstrete area appears to have been continuous. The line of Wansdyke, a Saxon earthwork of major importance, runs to the north incorporating the aforementioned hill fort at Stantonbury. The purpose of this has provoked much research and debate, with no definitive conclusion having been reached.

There is a strong possibility that the villages of Marksbury, Priston, Corston and Stanton Prior are based around the fort and the connecting roads that passed through the district. Marksbury derives its name from the Old English *mearc,* a boundary, and *burh,* a stronghold, suggesting that local communities were still very much in existence.

The first direct reference to Hunstrete, though not by name, is found in an Anglo Saxon charter of AD936. This records the grant of a piece of land at Merkesburi (Marksbury) by King Athelstan, to the thegn or nobleman Ethelelm, who was his son. The boundaries of this are described in great detail and many of them can still be identified today (for full description see appendix 1). They encompassed the present hamlet and included a reference to the boundary game enclosure, suggesting that a deer park was already established on the site. This further supports the theory of continued occupation, as buildings would have been necessary to house those involved with the management of the deer.

It seems likely that the document in question is actually a 12th century copy of the original, although Costen, in 'The Saxon Charters of Somerset', has suggested as late as 14th century based on the wording. The use of the name 'conigrave', meaning rabbit grove, tells us that it cannot be earlier than 1066 as this species was unknown in Britain, until brought here by the Normans. However it appears, in essence, the same as that of the 10th century, corresponding with the bounds of Stanton Prior and Priston where they meet, both of whose charters are known to be earlier.

The Mediaeval Period

Not long after this the land was given to the Abbey of Glastonbury, then the most important monastery in the country. They retained it for the next 600 years, apart from a brief period during the Danish wars of the mid 10th century, until the suppression of the monasteries in 1539. It is extremely unlikely that the monks ever lived there, instead letting it to tenants, thereby deriving an income from the estate.

The Domesday Book, the survey of land and property compiled for William the Conqueror in 1068, after the Norman invasion of England, provides the next piece of written evidence about Hunstrete. It states

> *The church itself holds Mercesberie. In the time of King Edward it gelded for ten hides Of this land a thane holds two hides and a half, It is worth twenty shillings, Oswald held it in the time of King Edward, and it could not be separated from the church.*

The two and a half hides referred to, approximating to 300 acres, was Hunstrete. At this time Marksbury was listed as having 40 acres of woodland, a considerable amount when much of lowland Britain had been cleared, and a valuable resource (for full Domesday entry see appendix 2).

Subsequent to this various references to the land appear in the abbey's documents and provide fascinating glimpses of its past. The following extract from the Glastonbury Chartulary, a record of abbey holdings, contains the first specific reference to Hunstrete by name, in the reign of Henry I (1100 - 1135). It reads

> *In the year of our Lord 1130 by the grace of God Abbot of Glastonbury with the consent and goodwill of the whole of the monastery of Glastonbury 3 virgatas in the manor of Merkesbury, in the place called Hundestert, to Lewin the son of Aylric of Bristol, to be held feely and in peace by him and his heirs; and in service for this land will give every year to the Brothers at Glastonbury 10 salmon in acknowledgement.*

This grant of land was confirmed by a charter of a subsequent king, Henry II, in 1153, which refers to Lewin as chamberlain to the Earl of Gloucester. It also mentions further tracts of land in Bristol, one of which may be the area now known as Lewin's Mead, together with Keynsham and Dundry. It was witnessed by, amongst others, Alexander Daundo, Lord of the Manor of Compton Dando. The rent of ten salmon was presumably to supply the abbey kitchens and had a monetary equivalent of five shillings.

The ruins of Glastonbury Abbey showing the Abbot's Kitchen in 1967

Lewin was one of many tenants that Hunstrete, together with its villeins and their brood, was leased to, over a long period of time, by Glastonbury Abbey. These were the unfree tenants and their families, bound to the land and required to give specified amounts of labour on the manor (for more information see chapter on Farming). Others included:

1189 Walter, son of Walter

1235 Lady Margeria de Hunderstert

1252 William Comyn who granted it to his son John. The Charter confirming this reads

Let all men present and future know that I William Comyn, Knight, Lord of Potelegh, Have given to my son John by my wife Emma for his service, 100 lb of silver, and the whole of my estate at Hundestert with buildings, gardens, etc. and all other holdings which I have in the County Of Somerset without any deduction

1305 John Comyn grants the manor of Hundestert to Nicholas de Chiltenham, clerk, who was the local clergyman. This included buildings, gardens, pasture and so on, together with all the villeins and their brood.

1310 Nicholas de Chiltenham grants the goods and chattels of Hundestert to his son John de Piggislegh, clerk, who was his son. He grants the manor itself to John de Jevele, with all its appurtenances including villeins and their brood. He in turn grants it to Geoffery, Abbot of Glastonbury, in frankalmoign; that is in return for prayers for his soul and those of his family and descendants.

1333 John de Piggislegh quitclaims to the Abbot of Glastonbury, all rights that his father, Nicholas de Chiltenham, once held in the manor of Hunstrete. He also renounced his entitlement to a yearly rent of 100 shillings, including any claims to arrears.

1339 John Comyn, lord of Piggeslegh, quitclaimed all rights he had in lands in Hundestert by gift of his father William, to John de Breinton, Abbot of Glastonbury.

During the two hundred years that the manor was rented to these tenants, a survey of monastic land in 1258 describes the area in detail and provides the first written evidence of a building on the site. It records a manor house, land and its usage including arable, pasture, meadow and wood, field names, rents both in money and kind and manorial service due from tenants. Collinson writing in 1791 in

'The History and Antiquities of the County of Somerset' gives us the following information regarding the value of the income from rents

In 1293 the temporalities of the abbey were valued at £15 10s. The Abbot had a charter of free warren in his lands within the manor by grant of King Edward.

Free warren was the sole right, granted by royal charter to a lord of the manor, to hunt within a given area. This applied to taking of pheasant, partridge, hare and rabbit. Most charters were granted between the late 12th and early 14th centuries.

It would appear that by now the Abbey of Glastonbury had acquired much surrounding land and property, including the manor of Chelworth or Chelwood. The estate seems to have been managed primarily for its deer park and its extensive woodlands, the latter occupying approximately a quarter of the land.

Early in the 14th century a cartulary or register taken of the abbey's possessions records a manor house with buildings, curtilage, lands, woods and pasture together with all the unfree tenants and their families. Sometime subsequent to this, during the time of Abbot Chinnock (1375 – 1420), the manor was rebuilt, as reported by the tenants in a survey of 1517. This was carried out by Thomas Sutton, cellarer to the abbey and contains statements, taken under oath, by John Phelps the manorial reeve and several of the tenants. It enthuses about the location of Hunstrete and the beautiful and delightful manor house. Part of it tells us what was there at this time

A chapel dedicated to the honour of St.Nicholas, a hall, chambers, buttery, kitchen, with a house on the south side of the hall called the gatehouse, a large stable and other outhouses; there were also orchards, gardens, and a desmene farm or barton. The manor house is environed with a great moat, filled by a rivulet and surrounded on all sides with oak pales, containing near two acres in circumference. The park adjoining to this house is deservedly esteemed one of the finest in the country.

Detail from the 1759 map (see page 6) possibly showing the building described in the 1517 survey

The survey also records the land and extensive woodlands at both Marksbury and Hunstrete. The woodland was carefully managed and provided a major source of income for the abbey. The manor continued to be rented, as were many other properties owned by Glastonbury, helping to defray the running costs of such a large establishment. The income from Hunstrete was used to support the cost of running the abbey kitchens, hence the involvement of the cellarer, who would have been responsible for supplies.

The Sixteenth Century

Life at Hunstrete continued in the early part of this century much as in the previous one. The Abbot of Glastonbury carried out a survey of his property in 1517, as denoted before, that provided glowing reports. However any complacency the abbey might feel was soon to be rudely awakened. Henry VIII's marital status and the ensuing break from the Catholic Church, were to have a marked effect on the fortunes of Hunstrete.

In 1539 the Abbey of Glastonbury, together with all its holdings, was forfeit to the crown as a result of the suppression of the monasteries. According to a survey taken at the time, and quoted in Collinson, the lands at Marksbury, including Hunstrete, were worth the following when returned

> *The rents assize and customary tennantes, apperteyning unto the said mannor, with the works and customes whiche by tenure of theire landes they are bound to doe are of a yerely value of £16 4s 5d.*
>
> *The demaye landes belonging unto the same manour are letton out by indenture for terme of yeres, for the some of £8 13s 6d.*
>
> *The profittes coming of the prequysites of courtes, fynes of landes, and other casualties, are this yere answered in the bokes of accompts at £4 4s 6d.*
>
> *Also there be within the same lordeships able men to doe the kings service, to the nombre of 17.*
>
> *Also there are apperteynyng unto the saide mannor, certayne woods, called Haywood, Newood, and the Common, set with okes and ashes of dyvers kyndes, the acres whereof cannot be esteemed, for they growe in plots, valued at this survey to be worth £106 19s 8d, whereof may be made a yerely wood sale of 60s.*
>
> *Also there is a common, apperteyning unto the sayde lordeship, wherein the tenanntes may put theire catle at theire pleasures, conteynyng 1 myle.*

The manors of Hunstrete and Marksbury and the advowson, or living, of the church at Marksbury were, according to Collinson, granted in 1543 to Richard

Watkins, alias Vaughan, of whose influence no trace can be found. Apparently various local families including the Thynnes of Longleat, the Hippisleys of Ston Easton, the Smyths of Ashton Court and the Pouletts of Hinton St George all had interests in the Hunstrete Estate during the latter part of the 16th century.

At the beginning of the 17th century the estate passed to the Popham family who held it for the next three hundred and fifty years. It may have been bought, or gifted to them in return for their services during the suppression of the monasteries, when they were appointed as bailiffs and receivers. This involved administering the winding up of monastic properties and wealth, in return for grants from the crown of land, annuities and other payments.

The Seventeenth Century

It is likely that the estate was acquired by Sir John Popham shortly before his death in 1607.The family already had interests in south Somerset, owning estates at Huntworth and Wellington, and was gradually acquiring land and property in the north of the county. Extensive searches of the Popham family papers have failed to provide direct evidence as to a specific date. However it can be confirmed as being in their possession by 1623, when a register of their land and properties, held in the British Museum, lists Hunstrete among their holdings. That Pophams were residing there soon afterwards, is proven by Aubrey, the 17th century biographer, who wrote of Sir John's only son and heir Sir Francis

> *Left by his father I thinke ten thousand pounds per annum he lived like a hog ...at Hunstrete*

Sir Francis died in 1644 and an inventory of the estate was compiled in 1646, a copy of which is displayed in the rear entrance hall of Hunstrete House. It makes fascinating reading and provides a room by room description of the manor house at that time, together with its outlying holdings. It comprised a great dining room, a hall, a

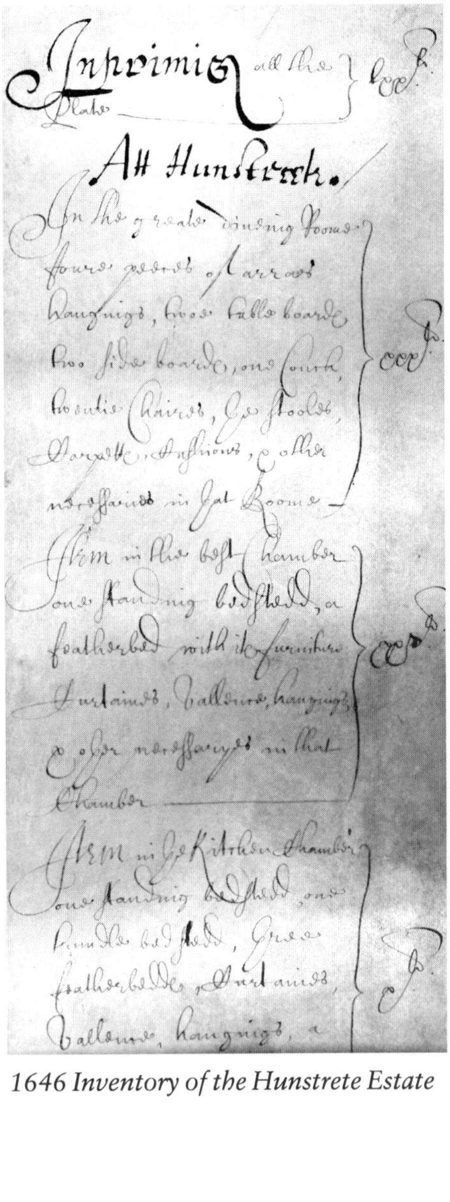

1646 Inventory of the Hunstrete Estate

gallery, eight chambers including a nursery and the Captaines Chamber with little chamber adjoining, a kitchen with larder and pantry, a wash house, a brew house and a porter's lodge with four chambers (for full inventory see appendix 3).

It corresponds, more or less, to the manor described in the Glastonbury Abbey survey of 1517. That is apart from the chapel to St. Nicholas, which is not mentioned, presumably because it was decommissioned at the time of the Reformation in 1539. The Captaines Chamber is assumed to be that of Sir Alexander Popham, a captain in the Parliamentary army.

What happened to Hunstrete after the demise of Sir Francis is unclear. His second son Alexander inherited, due to the death, in infancy, of his elder brother John. He seems to have lived mainly at Littlecote, the Popham seat in Wiltshire, although he is known to have resided at Hunstrete from time to time. The estate appears to have remained much as it was for the next fifty years. Exactly what buildings there were at this time is uncertain. The evidence, in the half yearly accounts, confirms that there were at least three in 1673, as there are payments to the chimney man for one half years duties for, amongst others, Houndstreet House, the new lodge and the old lodge.

The Eighteenth Century

At the beginning of the 18th century the estate underwent a period of change. A lease of 1702, for a period of seven years to Richard Cottle, refers to a new building at Hunstrete of which new stables were the north west part

> *All that part or appartment of the new building at Hounstreet aforesaid otherwise called the new stables being the north west part thereof containing one stable and hay room and four lodging rooms one story over the said stable and all the lodging rooms in the second story over the said stable and the still house and rooms within the still house yard and all that outlet used for feeding of pigs and poultry with the use of that courtyard to hold and keep wood and coal and the barnes and ox house near adjoining, and also two gardens called by the name of my Ladys gardens and the kitchen garden and the use in common of the outlet before the manor house of Hounstreet.*

Other leases for the same building were to John Cox of Long Ashton in 1709 and to John Moore of Hunstrete in 1731.

Where this new building was is the subject of debate. The earliest known map of the estate was drawn by John Hinde in 1759 (see page 6) and appears to show, in elevation form, the rebuilt manor of the late 14th century to the north and this later building to the west. It is difficult to interpret, being both very faint and heavily altered; the result of its apparent use as the basis of later plans. The western range looks to be a three-storey building, corresponding with the reference to *two storeys of lodgings over the new stables*, referred to in the lease.

In 1705 there were repairs to the lodge, brew house and stables and in 1707 there is one of many payments in the accounts for window tax. This was a form of revenue collection introduced in 1697. The occupier of every house was taxed at the rate of two shillings a year, with an additional payment of eight shillings for a house with over ten windows. In 1709 the rates were increased for larger properties and were frequently raised, until the abolition of the tax in 1851.

Also in 1707 there is a further reference to the old lodge and the new lodge. The former may well be the porter's lodge, containing four chambers with eight beds therein, mentioned in the inventory of 1646. The latter could be the building that forms the core of the present Hunstrete House, although there are problems with this theory, which I have discussed later in the chapter. In 1710 there is a payment for painting the windows of the great house.

Little appears to have happened during the next 50 years or so. A lease of 1755 tells us that besides Hunstrete House the estate included *gardens, orchards, fishponds, outhouses, the park and warren and lodges and lodgehouses.* On the 1759 map there is one building to the east of the main complex, with a small avenue of trees leading up to it, which I have taken to be the old lodge (see page 6).

Sometime after the mid 18th century, according to a note found on a statement of title and repairs of 1831, a decision was taken to demolish the mediaeval manor house and build in its place

> *A mansion on a most grand and magnificent scale*

Whether the idea for the new mansion was attributable to Edward Popham, his son Francis, or both, is debatable. The likelihood is that father and son discussed the venture and that Francis, not wanting to upset his elderly father, instigated the project after Edward's death in 1772. This seems to be borne out by the fact that the Grand Mansion features prominently in the background of a portrait of Francis, suggesting it was his dream (see illustration opposite).

Furthermore a bill of May 1771 exists for glazing at the great house and lodge and mending the guttering at the latter. These improvements probably wouldn't have been carried out, had the plans for the new house been in place.

Initially the old house and its associated buildings had to be demolished and the site cleared and levelled. As the planned Grand Mansion was so immense, part of the earth bank to the south of the site was cut away to form a large terrace. Archaeological excavations, undertaken in 1994 before the lake was extended, indicate that the red marl soil from here was dumped to the north of the building, where the fishing complex is now. All this would have taken a considerable amount of time and effort. Where Francis and Dorothy Popham were living at this time is unclear, but it may have been in a lodge, or possibly at Littlecote.

A lease of 1788 states that on 27th to 28th April 1755 Edward Popham granted to Richard Blake of Bristol, salesman

> *All that capital messuage or mansion house called Houndstreet house since pulled down and a new mansion house erected on the Grounds and Soil thereof*

Portrait of Francis Popham (1734-1780) with the Grand Mansion featuring in the background

This confirms that demolition and clearance of the old house had taken place by this date, although the reference to a new mansion erected on the same site is puzzling. Building work had probably only just started by 1788, so I assume this to mean intention, rather than achievement, in order for the lease to make sense.

A document of 1706 reveals that a bond existed for a debt, owed by Edward Popham, to the same Richard Blake of Bristol, salesman. What this was for is uncertain, as is whether it had any connection to the demolition or rebuilding work.

When the construction of the Grand Mansion commenced is not known. It would seem to be in the late 1770's, probably after the death of Edward Popham in 1772 and the demolition and clearance of the previous buildings on the site. Francis never lived to see his dream reach fulfilment, dying shortly after this in 1780. However his wife Dorothy, who must have been a very determined and strong willed lady, vowed to continue with the building. Her steward, Daniel Green, wrote to her in 1782, which suggests that she was indeed living elsewhere at the time, stating

> *The building goon very well at Houndstreet*

No formal plans have been found for the Grand Mansion and no architect has been identified although Beckford was suggested by the Reverend James Shepherd in 'Reminiscences of Prior Park College' written in 1886. It is possible that none existed and that the builder worked to his own drawings or that of his employer.

Paintings of the Grand Mansion, date and artist unknown, showing the north front above and the east front below

Until recently the only known evidence, as to its design, was the small background feature in the previously mentioned portrait. However, during the course of my research, I obtained a copy of a drawing of the Grand Mansion, by the Reverend Edward Langford, rector of Marksbury in the 1830's. This was reproduced in an article on Hunstrete by Michael McGarvie in 'Somerset and Dorset Notes and Queries'.

Langford's drawing of the Grand Mansion

I then received information that paintings of the Grand Mansion were thought to exist. Further enquiries led me to these, which are in the ownership of a member of the Popham family, who had always understood that they were architect's drawings. Whether that is so, or whether they were painted as representations of the north and east aspects of the house, is uncertain. The Royal Society of Architects suggested that they were artistic impressions, showing what the house would look like when complete. I find it strange that the fronts depicted were the only ones actually built. It is apparent that Langford's drawing was copied from one of these paintings, as it corresponds closely to the original.

On the back of one of the paintings, unbelievably, were the dimensions of the house, which had become visible in the dry summer of 1926 and had fortuitously, been recorded for posterity. These give the length as 200 feet and the width as 120 feet, a size that had it been completed, would have made it one of the largest mansions in the country. It was no doubt planned to impress and entertain the Popham family's guests, when a visit to Georgian Bath, at its fashionable height, was an essential part of high society's social calendar.

The five arches in the park, which once formed part of the Grand Mansion, reveal that it was constructed of coarse stone, faced with ashlar; a common practice to reduce building costs. The rectangular blocks were cut from freestone, also known as Bath Stone. It was so named from its widespread use in many of the buildings in that city and the surrounding area, particularly in the Georgian Period. It was mined extensively from quarries at Coombe Down on the outskirts of Bath and at Corsham and Box in Wiltshire.

In the accounts for 1788 is a payment for the carriage of freestone, this being a synonym for the same material. It is also known as oolitic limestone, so named from the small grains of calcium carbonate of which it is composed. These are called ooliths, from the Greek *oon* meaning an egg and *lithos*, a stone, from their strong resemblance to fish roe. When underground the stone is a mellow yellow and soft enough to be cut with a handsaw. It can be worked in any direction without regard to cracks or joints. On exposure to the atmosphere it hardens and becomes greyer in colour.

The accounts also give us glimpses of the planned design and particular features of the Grand Mansion

A bill of January 1783 refers to:
The cov'd room
The columd parlour
The octagon collum'd hall
And 76 ¾ square of blue tiling

In 1786 the plumber's account mentions
Items for the brew house and a water closet

The glazier's bill of 1788 lists
Skylights, casements and sash squares

In 1794 a payment was made for
Paving the laundry and wash house

Other surviving bills from the building of the Grand Mansion also give us an insight into the scale of the building, the amounts of materials purchased, the type and degree of labour involved and an idea of the costs incurred. Examples being:

1788 *a tun of alabaster*
lodging for plumbers
2000 tiles

1789 *a pound of hare for plastars brushes*
wages for Mr Sutton for turning caps and bases for colloms
2050 tiles

1790 *pan tiles*
payment of £1 0s 0d for 6 full worked pattern bannisters nicely turned to pattern drawings

1791 *wages for carving 65 banstars*
payment for work at the new stables

1792 *payment of £30 10s 0d for turning nicely to pattern the large mahogany bannisters for the grand staircase*
freestone for the new stables

1793 *payment for turning the caps and bases for chimley pics in the library*
settlement of an account for 4 lion masks and frames and for a chimney piece for the library
freestone for the new stables
a year's wages to the mason for building the new stables
payment to the surveyor for measuring and settling the carv'd work at Houndstreet. This included 138' of ogee mould with gothic band of flowers at 2s 6d per foot, 94' of small ogee with small leaf at 8d per foot, 1 doz of splatt back chairs with water leaf and flowers at 5d each and 2 ancient Ionic Coppes.

1794 *bill for slates*

The new stables are most likely to be the separate block to the east of the main hotel, now used as guest accommodation.

Other payments exist for:

> *green cloth for the billiard table, for one set of billiard balls, for the making of 24 mahogany chars, for a top for the door in the grand starcase and for a mortice lock for the mahogany doors*

Each provides us with a tantalising glimpse into the past and the furnishing of Francis Popham's Grand Mansion.

This documentation from the Popham family papers, together with accounts by Skinner (see page 25) and the evidence at Prior Park (see later in this section and separate chapter on Prior Park) enables us to establish a fair idea of what the Grand Mansion was like. This is further enhanced by the paintings of the building.

In 1797 Dorothy's death seems to have heralded the end of the building work. The project had been under way for approximately 27 years with

> *only the north and east fronts erected and these incomplete.*

The sheer scale of the undertaking and the enormous costs involved, not just for the Grand Mansion but for additional landscaping and so on, seems to have been its downfall. The incomplete building appears to have become a huge burden on the estate. Dorothy died childless and in her will left Hunstrete to the 'reputed son' of her husband, Francis (for full contents of will see Appendix 4). Whether he lived there is unclear, but he only survived her by a few years.

The Nineteenth Century

In 1804 the estate passed, through the female line, to the Leyborne family, on condition they assume the name and arms of Popham. The inheritor, Edward William Leyborne Popham, more commonly known as 'The General' seems to have initially lived at Littlecote and the Grand Mansion was left empty.

Here the situation becomes somewhat confusing. In 1806 a building called The Lodge was put up for rent, being advertised as

> *A capital, commodious and elegant stone mansion with its offices, stabling etc. with a lawn to the front and yards.*

In 1812 it was referred to as Hunstrete House, as a bill for repairing the windows confirms. In the same year slates were purchased to repair the stables.

However, the 1759 estate map appears to show no building on the site of the present house and I can only assume that it was constructed subsequent to this, or that it has been drawn over. The alterations to the original map make this very difficult to determine. In 1828 there are references to the old map and the new map. I have taken this to mean the 1759 map, and the date of the alterations made on it at a later date, probably when General Popham decide to live at Hunstrete.

Possibly the lodge was built as somewhere for Francis and Dorothy Popham to live whilst the Grand Mansion was being erected. Whatever the case I disagree with previous conclusions, often repeated in print, that Hunstrete House was constructed out of the stables and living quarters of outdoor staff. This refers to the building of 1702, of which *new stables with two storeys of lodgings over* formed the north west part. I believe this to be the western range of the mediaeval manor.

Meanwhile the Grand Mansion remained uninhabited. On 24th May 1822 the Reverend John Skinner, rector of Camerton and noted antiquarian, recorded in his diary

> *About five o'clock we left our Caravansary, and drove to Houndstreet Park, in order to visit the magnificent seat of General Popham.*
>
> *Although upwards of Thirty thousand Pounds were expended on the Mansion and grounds, not many years since, the whole is going fast to decay; there being no inhabitant on the premises, not even a person to open the windows. The noble piece of water is covered with weeds and long grass; thistles and nettles cover the walks: I can only regret these things as a passing traveller; but to those who reside in the vicinity, the blockade of such a residence as this must be severely felt, especially when all this money collected on the estate is compelled to flow into other channels. The evening was in every respect beautiful, and the setting sun*

> *one of the grandest I almost remember to have witnessed. We arrived at Radstock a little after nine highly gratified by our excursion.*

On 30th July 1828 he paid a second visit and confirmed his earlier prognosis

> *Admitted to the grand mansion, the interior of which especially the saloon, staircase, library and two other rooms, are fitted up with great care and cost, three Italians having been occupied on the work for several years. The ceilings are coved, and covered with a profusion of arabesque ornaments, painted in various colours; some in stucco, others carved in wood by the hand, which must have been a prodigious labour. The floorings are of fine grained oak, the banisters of the staircase, inlaid mahogany. The furniture has been removed by General Popham, the owner of the property, to his house at Littlecote, where he now resides; and it is reported that the house on which upwards of £60,000 was expended, will be pulled down. Already the silent destroyer rain has commenced its operations on the beautiful ceiling of the larger room, and thrown down a portion of the stucco ornaments, leaving the bare lathes. The outside of the mansion, which is of stone, I have before given in my sketches: on one of the pediments is sculpted the combat between Turnus and Aneas. Antique figures are introduced in niches, indeed altogether it is a magnificent place, commanding wood, water, and an extensive Park.*

These entries show the rapid deterioration of the building.

In the 1820's the Leyborne Pophams decided to extend the building referred to as The Lodge. It is this, much altered, which is the core of the present Hunstrete House. It occupies the north west corner and can be identified, from the exterior, by its pairs of smaller windows. Internally, a change in the upper floor level, together

Hunstrete House from the south showing the Georgian front

Hunstrete House from the west showing the Georgian front, identified by the larger windows

with higher ceilings at the front of the house, indicates a major alteration to the building. This was the addition of a Georgian frontage, complete with cellars. It took some 12 years to complete, as the documentary evidence detailed below reveals

1820 *A bill for hauling building materials for the new house*

1831 *A bill for a dressing room*
Payment to the architect
A reference to the cleaning of the new house

1832 *A bill for house and window tax on the new house at Hunstrete*

This relatively later part forms the south facing front aspect and part of the west side. The main doorcase from the Grand Mansion, was incorporated into the new building to form an imposing entrance, although the coat of arms on the over pediment must have been commissioned at this time, depicting as it does the Leybourne Popham quartering. Interior mahogany doors were also reused, suggesting that the General had no intention of using the old building as a residence. Indeed, rumour has it that when his wife was asked to state her preference, as to where to live, she chose the Lodge over Littlecote and the Grand Mansion.

In 1831 General Popham commissioned a survey of the Grand Mansion. This found dry rot, collapsed ceilings, floors giving way and deteriorating ornamental work (for full account see appendix 5).

It concluded the following:

To put the building in a secure state £5 000+
To put into perfect repair and restore the ornamental work £15 000+

To perfect the original design £60 000+
To demolish the said mansion and sort the material into saleable lots £500 - £600, the value of these being about £6 800.

The General, faced with such massive expenditure, and knowing the dilapidated condition of many of the buildings on the estate, opted for demolition, with the proceeds of the sale being used to build new farmhouses in the local area.

The main entrance to Hunstrete House incorporating a doorway from the Grand Mansion

The dismantling of the Grand Mansion duly took place and must have been completed by 1836 when the Catholic Bishop Baines, of Prior Park in Bath, purchased much of the materials. He intended to use them to refurbish his mansion, following its destruction by fire earlier that year (for a fuller account see chapter on Prior Park).

This fortuitous turn of events led to many features from the Grand Mansion being preserved. These included the ornamental plasterwork, doorcases, mahogany doors, fireplaces, a magnificent staircase and statues. Many of these were subsequently destroyed in a second fire at Prior Park in 1991 but have been sympathetically restored. After the Bishop's death the material, which had proved surplus to requirements, was sold. The sale catalogue provides an insight in to the sheer volumes involved, bearing in mind that much had already been appropriated (for full contents see appendix 6).

All that visibly remains of the former building, in situ, are the five central arches of what was a front portico. These were left as a romantic ruin and stand close to the lake, ironically a folly in both name and nature. To the north, a short distance away, part of what are presumed to be the cellars were discovered when a tractor fell into a hole in the 1980's. This has since been filled in.

A new waggon house was constructed in 1824 at a cost of £11 8s 2d. This is the building on the right, before the archway, when approaching the rear of the hotel from the car park. In the first part of the 20th century it was used as a barn and woodshed. It is now a store and a repair workshop.

Further alterations to Hunstrete House took place at the end of the 19th century. An article in a book about country houses, dated 1900, states that Francis William Leyborne Popham, who inherited in 1881, carried out considerable additions and improvements in 1890

> *Now the main entrance divides the original block from the modern extensions at the north east end, where he converted a coach house and stables into a gardener's cottage adjoining the main building ... the old orangery has been transformed into excellent garage and stables.*

The alterations all took place in the block to the east of the main house. An inventory of 1891 gives a detailed list of all the rooms in the house at this time (for full details see appendix 7). It informs us that there were ten bedrooms in Hunstrete House, plus three bedrooms over the coach house and stables mentioned above. These were for outdoor staff and were still there in the 1970's, although somewhat dilapidated.

Courtyard doorway and window above, which may have been part of the orangery

The above quote is the only reference I have come across to Hunstrete having an orangery. However the shape of many of the present windows is consistent with this statement, being similar in design to ones still in existence in other country houses. As orangeries need a great deal of light, and there were apparently no windows on the east side of the building, at that time, I am still uncertain as to the exact nature of it.

It was probably during the course of these renovations, that the structure outside the garden door to the bar was removed. It appears on 19th century maps and

A family group, photographed in the early twentieth century, showing the lighter stonework where a conservatory was probably attached to the house

photographs taken in the early part of the 20th century show paler stonework, where it was attached to the main building. It is most likely to be the conservatory listed in the 1891 inventory. The stonework is now hidden behind foliage.

The Twentieth Century

The house seems to have survived in this form, with minor additions and alterations, for the greater part of the 20th century. Sales of land and property, in the surrounding area, took place in 1911 and 1917. These were probably to finance the running of the estate and to settle some of the debts left by Francis William Leyborne Popham.

The laundry room (now Swallow) still had its original fitments, in the first half of the 20th century. Gillian Barnes, who lived in the gardener's cottage as a child in the 1940's, recalls it was disused in her day, but intact. She described a row of wooden wash tubs on the ground floor, situated along the window wall and on the first floor a large clothes - drying room. This was used as an apple store. There was also a pump outside, the stone trough for which is still there.

In the 1940's the estate passed, again through the female line, to Major Eric Buller Leyborne Popham, a cousin. In 1956 the prohibitive running costs forced its sale, so bringing to an end the 350 year long association of the Pophams with Hunstrete. It had only changed hands twice in over 1 000 years, a feat matched by few other country estates. It was bought by Sir Christopher and Lady Chancellor, who lived in it as a family home, virtually unaltered, for the next 20 years.

It was then sold in 1977 to John and Thea Dupays who converted it to a hotel. They created 13 en suite bedrooms in the main house, naming them after species of bird. They added a new kitchen and built a restaurant in what was a grassed courtyard. The former laundry and gardener's accommodation was converted to three cottages, one for themselves and two for staff. This earned the Dupays a Countryside Landowners Association award, for the conversion of a derelict building and the provision of rural employment, which was presented at Highgrove by Prince Charles.

They retained the stables and decided to resurface the large courtyard as it was part cobbled, with the remainder rough stone. Madame Tussauds in London, of waxworks fame, purchased the cobbles for use in the recreation of a mediaeval street scene.

The Dupays eventually built up the number of bedrooms to 24, by using the staff cottages. These were replaced by purpose built accommodation for the hotel employees. They also linked the main house with the outbuildings by adding a corridor along the north wing and an additional room, used by Mrs Dupays as an art studio, joined to the main building by an arch. This meant that movement right round the complex could take place under cover.

Two of their original staff still work at Hunstrete House. Ahmed Asri, who runs the bar, came with them from their previous hotel, the Priory in Bath, and Mike Marsh the gardener, who they employed during their first year. Sheila Duckett, the housekeeper, who retired in 2003, worked at Hunstrete for 25 years. She had previously worked for the Chancellors and stayed on with the Dupays.

During their ownership Captain Douglas White, an old friend, made the following discovery. I quote from his account

> *Set in the south wall in the main courtyard is a stone, unusual by its size, curved face and rounded top against the rough stone of the wall itself. It bears an all but illegible inscription of which only an occasional word can be distinguished and its style suggests a memorial stone, but nobody could say to whom or why it was there. It was only the other day that I solved our small mystery. Early last year improvements were made to the courtyard and new lighting was installed, including a light close to*

one side of the stone. With the coming of early darkness in October the light showed, unexpectedly, shadows in the depressions of the lettering of the inscription which was enough to make most of it readable. I realised that it is part of the inscription on a memorial in Marksbury Church, a mile away. In the grandiose style of the times it reads as follows:

To the memory of Francis Popham Esq, eldest son of Edward Popham one of the representatives in several Parliaments for the county of Wilts; descended from Lord Chief Justice Popham and heir to the fortunes as well as the virtues of a family distinguished to the interests of their country. This monument is erected by his widow in testimony of her affection.

Ob. 4 Feb 1779 Aet 45

The assumption is that this stone was removed from Marksbury church and placed here after his widow Dorothy's death in 1797. A far more elaborate memorial, to them both, was then erected at the church (for full inscription see chapter on The Popham Legacy). The courtyard stone is now virtually indecipherable due to the ravages of time and weather.

Detail from the Italian fountain

Also in this courtyard Mrs Dupays placed, as a central feature, a large, elaborate, Italian ornamental fountain. This proved to be another victim of the weather, irreparably damaged due to the expansion of frozen water, when it was left filled during one winter, after they had sold the hotel. One part of it stands outside the entrance to Robin, whilst others are scattered throughout the gardens and grounds.

In 1989 the Dupays sold Hunstrete House and it has passed through the hands of several hotel chains since. However only minor alterations took place at the end of the 20th century. This was mainly a reduction in the number of bedrooms from 24 to 22.

The Twenty First Century

There is an ongoing programme of development and in 2002 the former staff block was converted to additional guest accommodation. Employees now live out in the local area.

The present hotel comprises 25 rooms, 14 twin, 11 double and three suites. Elizabeth Lloyd, formerly Leyborne Popham, who grew up in the house, told me the function of some of the rooms in the 1930's:

Jay - main guest room
Dove - her parents' room
Heron - dressing room
Kingfisher - the night nursery (later her sister Ann's room)

The gardens are undergoing total renovation, a project that was started in 2001 and should be completed by the end of 2004. A new stable block was constructed in 2002, adjacent to the site of the former pigsties, to house the Glen Eyr stud of Haflinger horses. Plans are currently being drawn up to extend the hotel's facilities to include a health spa in the grounds. An orangery is also to be built. Hunstrete House is currently a Grade II listed building (see Appendix 8).

Aerial view of Hunstrete House

Prior Park

Prior Park is situated at the top of a picturesque valley overlooking the city of Bath. It was built for Ralph Allen, the founder of the modern postal service, being designed by John Wood the Elder. Planning commenced in 1728 but the start of construction was delayed until 1734. In 1829 the house was purchased by Bishop Baines to found a seminary and Roman Catholic college.

In 1836 a serious fire destroyed much of it. Bishop Baines set about the task of rebuilding and for this purpose purchased the materials and contents of the Grand Mansion at Hunstrete, although whether this was prior to, or after, demolition is unclear. It would appear that he bought the building in its entirety.

Mahogony door from the Grand Mansion at Hunstrete

Eason in 'Georgian Buildings of Bath' gives the following description after the restoration was complete

The interior decoration was designed to incorporate many beautiful specimens of late eighteenth -century decorative art, including a magnificent staircase in oak and mahogany; several sets of fine mahogany veneered doors, some richly carved doorcases, pilasters, and cornices; mantlepieces in marble and wood, and a series of plasterwork panels and ceiling centrepieces of markedly similar character to the work in Baldwin's Guildhall.

As the building of the Guildhall was contemporary with the Grand Mansion, being constructed in 1776, it is possible that the same plasterers were used. The article continues

> *All of this material was brought from Hunstrete, near Marksbury, when the great mansion built by Francis Popham was dismantled. From this house came also the vigorous sculptures now ornamenting the tympanum of the east wing pediment, together with two oval medallions on either side of the venetian window below, and some statues ranged about the portico and terraces.*

In 1931, J.S. Roche writing a history of Prior Park provides us with an amusing anecdote regarding the statues from Hunstrete. These appear to be those adorning the exterior of the Grand Mansion and were designed to occupy purpose built niches (see illustrations on page 20).

Four pagan statues also came from Houndstreet House, and by the skill of the Thewetti brothers and the devices of Dr. Baines, the statues were converted by means of cement and plaster into Popes and Saints. They for some time adorned the front steps, but as the weather proved too great a strain for their veneer of sanctity, the converts soon returned to their pagan state - with the exception some say of the mitres and tiaras, which retained their positions! These were forcibly removed and the statues as originally carved now adorn various parts of the building in full harmony with their classic surroundings.

Statue from the Grand mansion

Unfortunately history repeated itself and in 1991 there was another serious fire at Prior Park, which destroyed much of the Hunstrete material. This was painstakingly restored by St. Blaise Limited, a company specialising in historic reconstruction. The plasterwork in particular, proved a great challenge. All the pieces from Hunstrete were readily identified, as they were found to be on a pinky backing plaster of sand and lime. To recreate the original composition, determined by chemical analysis, a large quantity of soil was removed from the bank adjacent to the site of the Grand Mansion. This proved that the original plasterwork was constructed on site, giving credence to the local legend that three Italian craftsmen were employed for seven years, entirely for this purpose, during the building of the Grand Mansion.

The plasterwork that had to be replaced comprised 26 ceiling coves, five doorcases, four medallions, three ceiling roses, modillions and pilasters. The painstaking rebuilding of the sequence of trophy panels, in the ceiling cove of the Academy Hall, was a noted success. It used any surviving fragments, these being skillfully incorporated, and was reconstructed through the use of photographs of the originals. The panels depict hunting, fighting, the arts and gardening. The hunting one involved particular skill, as its centrepiece was a stag's head with points, similar to that in the Popham crest.

According to an article in Country Life magazine, a probable link was established between the Hunstrete plasterwork and the plasterer William Collins. This was due to the discovery that parts of it appeared to exactly match a set of wall medallions at Burton Constable in Humberside, where he was known to have worked. So maybe the story of the Italian craftsmen is legend after all and the link with Baldwin at the Guildhall tenuous.

Planning the restoration of the hunting panel in the Academy Hall at Prior Park

The restored panels depicting hunting and the arts, formerly in the Grand Mansion at Hunstrete

Certainly the grand mahogany staircase, reused at Prior Park, was created by British craftsmen as several bills exist for, amongst other elements, the carving of *balustars*. However this was entirely destroyed in the fire and was totally reconstructed from photographs.

The restoration took almost four years with Prior Park reopening in 1995. The building continues to function as a private school and is not open to the public. However the grounds are now owned by the National Trust and are accessible on foot.

Details of the restored mahogany staircase at Prior Park. The original came from the Grand Mansion at Hunstrete

Owners of the Hunstrete Estate

936	Ethelelm
c 963	Glastonbury Abbey
1543	Watkins
c 1600	Sir John Popham
1607	Sir Frances Popham
1644	Alexander Popham
1669	Sir Francis Popham
1674	Alexander Popham
1705	Alexander Popham
1705	Francis Popham
1736	Edward Popham
1772	Francis Popham (from 1780 his wife Dorothy)
1797	Francis Popham
1804	Edward William Leyborne Popham
1843	Francis Leyborne Popham
1881	Francis William Leyborne Popham
1907	Hugh Francis Leyborne Popham
1943	Eric Tremayne Buller Leyborne Popham
1956	Sir Christopher and Lady Chancellor
1977	John and Thea Dupays
1989	Clipper Hotels
1991	Arcadian Hotels
1996	Furlong Hotels
1998	North American Country Inns

Popham Owners of Hunstrete

The Popham Family

The Popham family originated from the hamlet of Popham some 10 miles north east of Winchester. The first known person to bear the title was Agnes de Popham who in 1189 adopted the name of her birthplace. The family came to Somerset when Hugh de Popham married Joane la Blanche, who had inherited Huntworth, near North Petherton. This branch of the family appear to have dropped the prefix 'de' about this time. Alexander Popham rebuilt the house on the same site about 1540. It passed out of the hands of the family in 1632, due to a debt, and was destroyed by fire in 1825.

Sir John Popham (1531 - 1607)

Sir John Popham was born at Huntworth, in Somerset, in 1531. He was the second son of Alexander Popham and Joan, the daughter of Sir Edward Stradling of St Donat's Castle in Glamorganshire. Whilst still a child the stories and rumours that were to persist throughout his life began. The following tale, recounted by Lord Campbell in his 'Lives of the Chief Justices' said of him

> *Whilst yet a child he was stolen by a band of gipsies, and remained some months in their society... his captors had disfigured him, and had burnt on his left arm a calabalistic mark, which he carried with him to the grave.*

As with most of the stories surrounding him, it has proved difficult to separate fact from fiction.

He was educated at Balliol College, Oxford reading Classics and Divinity. He then moved to the Middle Temple in London to qualify as a lawyer, where he reputedly got into bad company and neglected his judicial studies. Tradition has it that he frequently sallied forth at night from a hotel in Southwark, with a band of desperate characters, and that planting themselves in ambush on Shooter's Hill, they stopped travellers, and took from them their money and valuables.

Aubrey, the 17th century biographer, attributes his reformation to the influence of his wife Amy, daughter of Robert Games of Glamorgan. He writes of him

> *For several yeares he addicted himself but little to the studie of the lawes, but profligate company, and was wont to take a purse with them. His wife considered her and his condition, and at last prevailed with him to lead another life, and to stick to the studie of the lawe, which, upon her opportunity, he did, beeing then about thirtie yeares ald. He spake to his wife to provide a very good entertainment for his camarades to take his leave of them, and after that day fell extremely hard to his studie, and profited exceedingly. He was a strong stout man, and could endure to sit at it day and night.*

They had seven children, six daughters and finally a son, born when his parents were in their forties. The family appears to have moved to Wellington in Somerset around this time and Sir John added to his land in the county, probably acquiring Hunstrete at the beginning of the 17th century. In the meantime Popham was making a name for himself and was well on the way, according to rumour, to creating the greatest fortune ever amassed by a lawyer called to the bar. In 1568, at the age of 37, he was nominated Reader at the Temple and 12 years later became treasurer. Meanwhile he had obtained a seat in Parliament as MP for Bristol. In 1579 he was appointed Solicitor General and whilst holding that office was elected Speaker of the House of Commons in January 1581. As such when attending Elizabeth I he is said to have taken part in the following exchange

> *The Queen ' Well, Mr Speaker, what hath passed in the lower house'*
>
> *Sir John Popham ' If it please your Majesty, seven weeks'*

In June of the same year he became Attorney General, an office he held for 11 years.

In 1592 he was elevated to Lord Chief Justice of the King's Bench and was knighted. He continued to hold that role until his death fifteen years later, serving both Queen Elizabeth I and King James I. As such he was notable for participating in a number of famous trials. He played a minor role in that of Mary Queen of Scots, but presided at the trial of Sir Walter Raleigh, in 1603, for his part in the plan to place Lady Arabella Stuart on the throne. Raleigh was found guilty and sentenced to death although this was later commuted to imprisonment; his ultimate execution taking place under the auspices of a later Chief Justice. One of the last trials Judge Popham presided over, in 1605, was the Gunpowder Plot, to blow up the Houses of Parliament and exterminate King James I in the process.

Sir John Popham was notorious as a harsh judge particularly against common felons and according to Fuller he recommended King James be more sparing in his pardons to the malefactors who then infested the highways. Dr Donne, the Dean of St Paul's Cathedral, wrote in a letter to Ben Johnson

> *With guilty conscience let me be worse stung*
> *Than with Popham's sentence, thieves.*

The Popham family were related to the Darrells of Littlecote in Wiltshire and Sir John was consulted by William Darrell, also known as 'Wild Darrell' in numerous legal matters, many involving disputes with neighbours. It is this relationship which gave rise to the most contentious episode in the judge's life. He was reputed to have acquired Littlecote as the result of a bribe, in return for Darrell escaping conviction in a murder trial (see chapter on Legends). Aubrey says of the event

> *That the Knight was brought to his Tryall and, to be short, that the Judge had his noble house, parke and manor to save Darrell's life.*

However the evidence contradicts this. Popham was not a judge until 1592 and the trial took place ten years earlier. It is more likely that Sir John either inherited Littlecote or that he purchased it. A bill of sale is said to be in the British Museum but I have been unable to trace it. The likely scenario, bearing in mind that most legends have some basis in truth, is that Popham gave his relation the benefit of his legal experience. As a result of this, they came to an arrangement about Littlecote on Darrell's death, there being no immediate heir.

Sir John Popham's most famous words were

> *Haste, haste I say - Haste, Post Haste - Haste*

This being the message he gave a Somerset horseman, to relay to the government in London, in 1588. A Bridgwater ship's captain, on the lookout for the Spanish fleet, had sighted it in the distance, thereby providing the first real news of the approaching Armada.

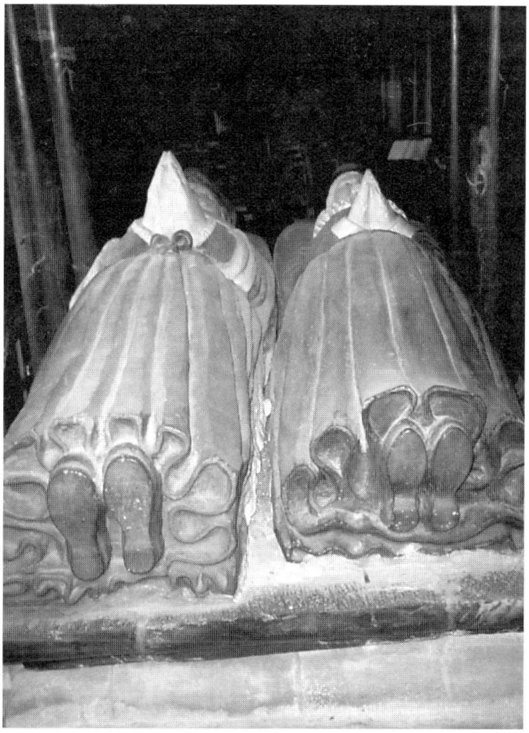

Effigies of Sir John Popham and his wife Amy, on their tomb in Wellington church

In 1586 Sir John became involved in Queen Elizabeth's scheme for the plantation of Munster. However his most memorable deed is, arguably, his sponsorship of an expedition to North America in 1607 that led to the founding of the Popham Colony. This was a speculative venture, involving his nephew George, that was ultimately to fail. It nevertheless introduced the name Popham to the New World (for further information see chapter on The American Connection).

In death Sir John remained as controversial as he had been in life. In 1607, aged 76, he disappeared whilst out hunting in the Blackdown hills. His horse returned to the stables without him and he was presumed to have met with an accident. The body was never found and a local place became known as Popham's pit. Rumours circulated that he had been murdered but nothing was ever proven. His name and effigy adorn an ornate family tomb in the parish church in Wellington. When this was relocated in 1938, Amy's remains were found but not those of her husband. Whether they were there when it was previously moved in 1848 is unknown.

Sir Francis Popham (1573 - 1644)

Sir Francis Popham was the only son and heir of Sir John Popham and his wife Amy, although he had six elder sisters. He followed in his father's footsteps matriculating at Balliol College, Oxford in 1588, aged 15, and a year later becoming a student at Middle Temple. In 1590, aged 17, he married Anne, daughter of John Dudley of Stoke Newington, by whom he had five sons and eight daughters.

In 1596 Francis accompanied the Earl of Essex on his expedition against the Spaniards and was present at the sacking of Cadiz, where Essex knighted him for his services. The following year he was elected MP for Somerset. He subsequently represented Wiltshire from 1604 - 1611, Marlborough in 1614, Great Bedwyn 1621 - 22, Chippenham 1625 - 29 and Minehead 1640, sitting in every parliament except the 'Short Parliament' of 1640. He supported its resistance to Charles I and when the crisis came in the 'Long Parliament' of 1640 he lent his support to John Pym in his condemnation of ship money and other taxes. He sided with the Parliamentarians when the situation eventually led to Civil War in 1642.

In 1607 he inherited his father's vast estates to become one of the wealthiest men in the West Country. Like his father he speculated in the colonisation of North America and was a member of the Council for both Virginia and New England. He also had financial interests in land in Ulster and Munster. He became Constable of Taunton Castle in 1620, was a Justice of the Peace from 1623 and from 1625 was Deputy Lieutenant of Somerset.

His eldest son John was born in 1603 and married Mary, daughter of Sebastian Harvey, Lord Mayor of London in 1618. They lived at Littlecote whilst Francis decamped to Hunstrete. John died in his father's lifetime and Aubrey says of him

> *He was the greatest howse - keeper in England:*
>
> *would have at Littlecote 4 or 5 or more lords at a time. His wife (Harvey) was worth to him, I thinke, £60 000, and she was as vaine as he, and she sayed that she had brought such an estate, and she scorned but she would live as high as he did; and in her husband's absence would have all the women of the countrey thither, and feast them, and make them drunke, as she would be herself. They both dyed by excesse; and by luxury and cosanage by their servants, when he dyed, there was, I thinke, a hundred pound debt.*

Meanwhile as Aubrey once again comments

> *Old Sir Francis, he lived like a hog at Houndstrete in Somerset, all this while with a moderate pitttance.*

One can imagine the gossips having a field day, discussing the antics of the Popham family. The following epitaph was written after John died in 1669

> *Here lies he who not long since*
> *Kept a table like a prince*
> *Til Death came and tooke away*
> *Then asked the old man "What's to pay?"*

Three of his other sons did much to restore the family reputation by giving service to their country. Alexander, his subsequent heir, and Hugh fought on the side of parliament in the Civil War. Hugh was killed in a skirmish with Royalist townsfolk at Sherborne in 1643, whilst Alexander distinguished himself as a Colonel. Edward joined the Navy and in 1649 was appointed Admiral and General At Sea. He gained notoriety when he led a troop of horse into the sea, which was at a low ebb due to the tide, and captured a ship, this incident taking place at Watchet, Somerset, during the Civil War. He died of a fever at Dover in 1651.

Sir Francis died at Stoke Newington in 1644 and was buried in the parish church there. Three years later his remains were removed to Bristol and reinterred in the Mayor's chapel of St Marks. Two years after his death an inventory was compiled of the estate at Hunstrete. In this Sir Francis is referred to as 'One of the Gentlemen of His Majesty's Privy Chamber' and as a Colonel of the Regiment of Foot in the County of Wiltshire. The original of this document is at present in private ownership.

Alexander Popham (1605 - 1669)

Alexander Popham was his father's second son, becoming heir on the death of his elder brother John. He was born in 1605 and also followed family tradition by matriculating at Balliol College, Oxford in 1621 and being admitted to the Middle Temple in 1622. He married, at the relatively late age of 30, Katherine, daughter of Richard Cole of Nailsea. By her he had a son Francis who died in infancy in 1642, followed by his wife in 1643. He then took as his second wife Letitia, daughter of William Carr. She was the sister of his brother Edward's wife. They had five sons and three daughters, the eldest son and heir being Francis, born in 1646.

He was elected MP for Bath in 1640 and held the seat until 1655. In 1644 he became a Commissioner for Martial Law and in 1650 one of the Council of State. In 1656 he was elected MP for Wiltshire but Cromwell suspecting him of leanings towards a Republican form of government, instead promoted him as a Lord in the Upper House. He inherited, on the death of his father in1644, large estates and was said to have enjoyed an income of £3 000 a year from Hunstrete alone.

He became a Colonel in the Parliamentary Army during the Civil War and as such was prominent in Cromwell's campaign in the Western Counties, until it ended with the surrender of Dunster castle in 1646. He used Hunstrete as a base for his troops, prior to joining his contemporaries, at Chewton Mendip in August 1642 (for a more detailed account see chapter on Hunstrete at War). He was again active in Somerset, in 1648, during the second Civil War, raising a troop of horse.

In 1659 he became MP for Minehead and was again appointed as a member of the Council of State from 1659 - 1660. He was elected to the Army Committee in 1659. After the fall of Cromwell he supported the Royalist cause, making his peace with Charles II who subsequently visited Littlecote in 1663. Following the Restoration he continued to sit in Parliament, again as MP for Bath, until his death in 1669. He was buried at Chilton Foliat, having lived most of his life at Littlecote, letting out Hunstrete to tenants. In his will he gives loving admonition to his children

> *I have made provision by my said settlement for my two younger sons in my eldest Son's marriage and I do require them to respect and reverence him as a Parent. I having hereby put him in my own stead; they to tread in the paths of their Mother, who is gone to bliss before them - my daughter in law, Dame Helena Popham - I desire my well beloved Brother in law, Henry Rogers of Cannington to give my son his counsel and assistance - £10 to my Brother to buy him a ring.*

Alexander adds that copies of the will are to be sent to them, and that they are to read it over once a month.

Sir Francis Popham (1646 - 1674)

Francis Popham was the eldest son of Alexander by his second wife. His son by his first wife, whom the couple had similarly named Francis, died in infancy. He was baptised at St Giles in the Fields in London and at the coronation of Charles II in 1660, was created a Knight of the Bath, aged 14. This was a purchased knighthood with the proceeds going to swell the coffers of the new King, as well as to buy his goodwill. His father had supported Cromwell for most of the Commonwealth period and was particularly anxious to court royal favour.

He married in 1668, Helena daughter and heiress of Hugh Rogers of Cannington near Bridgewater and by her had two children, Alexander and Letitia. Their mother died in 1672 and in 1674 their father, leaving the five year old boy and three year old girl in the care of their Aunt, Letitia Popham. As the children were baptised at Chilton Foliat and their parents buried there, it is presumed they were living at Littlecote at that time. There appears to be no record of them having spent any considerable length of time at Hunstrete and leases show that it was let at this time.

Alexander Popham (1669 - 1705)

Alexander was a minor when he inherited, being aged five when his father died in 1674. He married Lady Ann Montagu, daughter of Ralph, 1st Duke of Montagu. They had one child Elizabeth. Alexander died intestate in 1705, aged 36, and the estates went to his uncle Alexander, the surviving brother of his father Francis. Again throughout his ownership Hunstrete appears to have been let.

Alexander Popham (1657 - 1705)

Alexander Popham came into the ownership of the estates on the death of his nephew. He had married Jane French and by her had four sons and two daughters. He was MP for Chippenham in 1689 and 1695 and for Bath in 1698, 1700 and 1705. As Alexander died within months of inheriting, the eldest son and heir Francis, followed on almost immediately. The two girls died childless, Ann in 1739 and Letitia in 1753. The second and third sons Edward and Alexander also died childless in 1783. Their death was particularly poignant with the parish register at Chilton Foliat recording

> *They died within thirty hours of each other, and were buryed both in the one grave.*

No reference is given as to the cause of death in either case, leaving the matter open to speculation. The remaining son George went on to become Rector of Chilton Foliat and also died without issue.

Again Hunstrete appears to have been leased out at this time.

Francis Popham (1682 - 1736)

Francis Popham was born in 1682, the eldest of six children. He married his second cousin Ann who died in childbirth in 1712, but not before giving him six children, two of whom Elizabeth and Francis, died in infancy. The remaining children were Alexander who died without issue in 1722, Ann who died unmarried in 1737, Letitia and Edward the heir, who was born in 1709. Francis was MP for Wootton Bassett, near Swindon, from 1706 - 1710. He died intestate in 1736.

Edward Popham (1709 - 1772)

Edward Popham inherited at the age of 27. He matriculated at Christ Church, Oxford in 1729. He became MP for Bedwyn in Wiltshire from 1734 - 1741 and for the next 31 years until his death in 1772 Member for the County of Wiltshire. He married Rebecca Huddon and they had three children. Francis born in 1734, Ann born in 1737 and Edward born in 1739. Their mother died in 1742 when all three were under eight years of age.

It seems that the family had begun to occupy Hunstrete again at this time and Edward may have been involved in the initial planning of the Grand Mansion.

Francis Popham (1734 - 1780)

Francis Popham the eldest son of Edward Popham was born in 1734. Like most of his predecessors he matriculated at Oxford. He married twice, firstly in 1772 a Mrs Wallace who was a widow and secondly Dorothy Hutton, daughter of the then Archbishop of Canterbury. Francis is generally attributed with being the instigator of the Grand Mansion at Hunstrete and indeed this appears in the background of a portrait of him(reproduced on page 19). However he died in 1780, only a few years after building had commenced. His wife, who apparently inherited the estate, continued with the task until her own demise in 1797.

He appears to have had no lawful issue, but in her will Dorothy bequeathed

> *All her manors at or near Hunstrete and Littlecote and all her property in Somerset, Wiltshire and Berkshire, which she had from her husband Francis, to his 'reputed' son Francis for life, subject to certain conditions, with remainder to his heirs male* (presumably in accordance with her late husband's wishes)*: whom failing however, to her sister-in-law, Ann Leyborne's son, Edward William Leyborne and his heirs male requiring that he take the surname and quarter the arms of Popham.*

Francis Popham (1770 - 1804)

Francis duly inherited and died without issue in 1804, so the estates did indeed pass through the female line to the Leybornes. Ann was the sister of Dorothy's husband Francis and had married William Leyborne Leyborne in 1763. He was appointed Governor of Grenada in 1772 and held that office until his death in 1775. They had three sons and a daughter, the eldest being Edward William.

Edward William Leyborne Popham (1764 - 1843)

Edward William Leyborne inherited in 1804 and duly assumed the name and arms of Popham by Royal patent. He was a soldier in the 24th regiment and ultimately attained the rank of General. He was also a Justice of the Peace for Wiltshire and in 1830 became High Sheriff. He married Elizabeth, daughter of Archdeacon Andrew in 1806. They had eight children, their son Edward William inheriting in 1843.

Edward William Leyborne Popham (1807 - 1881)

Edward William Leyborne Popham's birth is recorded in the parish registers of Marksbury church as follows

> *1807 Born at Hunstrete in ye county of Somerset on ye 6th day of Sept in ye same year aboute 10' clock in ye morn*

He appears to have lived all his adult life at Littlecote as a recluse and died without issue in 1881. He collected a considerable amount of silver and directed, by a codicil to his will in 1843, that this be added to the 'Popham Plate'. He also requested that an inventory be made of this, for the better information of his heirs. Much of this was sold in 1891 (for further details see appendix 9).

Francis William Leyborne Popham (1862 - 1907)

Francis William Leyborne Popham was born in 1862. He was one of six children, two girls and four boys, of which the eldest Francis Hugh died in infancy. He was educated at Harrow and Oxford. In 1881, at the age of 19, he inherited the family estates, together with a great deal of money from his father's brother Edward William Leyborne Popham. In 1890 he married Maud Isabel, daughter of Henry Howard of Greystoke Castle in Northumberland.

His chief pleasures were travelling and sailing. He was also a self taught violinist, with a great love of music. He spent his inheritance on wild schemes including the building of yachts, constructing Lewes racecourse and the development of a pier at Southampton. At the end of the 19th century and in the early part of the next, Francis compiled various inventories of furniture, china, glass, linen, the contents of the wine cellar, silver and jewellery (for further details see appendix 10). At this time he had considerable debts and was no doubt realising his assets, as a sale of fine wines in 1892, held at the Grand Hotel in Bristol, reveals. In 1900 he also sold some of the family silver and a tiara in the shape of a flower wreath, composed of brilliants and rose diamonds, which achieved the sum of £325.

In order to save Littlecote and Hunstrete he made a financial arrangement with his brother in law Arthur Treymayne Buller. Being childless, he agreed that on his death the estates should pass first to his younger brother Hugh and subsequently to Eric, who was the son of Arthur and Francis' second sister Elinor Louise. He ultimately separated from his wife, who returned to her family home. Suffering from tuberculosis, he moved to the Isle of Wight, where he died in 1907.

Hugh Francis Leyborne Popham (1864 - 1943)

Hugh Francis Leyborne Popham was born in 1864 and was educated at Cheltenham and Brasenose College, Oxford. He then took rooms in London. He inherited the family estates on the death of his elder brother Francis William, who died childless, in 1907. He married Janet Emily, eldest daughter of Freeman William Hunt of Plymouth, the following year at the age of 44, and they moved into Hunstrete. They had five children: Elizabeth Marjorie, Mary Frances and Letitia Ann together with Janet Maud and John Hugh both of whom died in infancy in 1910 and 1912 respectively.

He travelled to Siberia in his brother's yacht, being a great sailor, and explored the mouths of the Ob and Yenisey rivers. At a meeting of the British Ornithological Union on 20th October 1897 he exhibited a clutch of four eggs of the curlew sandpiper; the first authentic breeding record. He had collected them from a nest, on the estuary of the river Yenisey, on 3rd July 1897, shooting the female bird in the process! He was shipwrecked three times in the White Sea and in the Kara Sea in 1894. He was rescued from here by Samoyeds, or Eskimoes, and lived in a tent with them for four months. He then drove a sledge to Moscow. He helped to establish a sea route to Siberia and open up its interior, risking capital to do so, which allowed trade to develop in the region. He kept diaries of his travels, which were later donated to the Scott Museum in Cambridge.

Hugh Leyborne Popham was passionately interested in ornithology, regularly sending sightings of the first migrants each year to 'The Field' magazine. From these the demise of birds at Hunstrete, such as turtle dove and wood warbler, can be deduced. He eventually became vice president of the British Ornithological Union.

He was a keen field sportsman regularly shooting both game and wildfowl and often travelled to Holland to pursue duck. He bred cattle, chickens and dogs and showed all three, many of which won prizes. Eventually the costs of running Hunstrete, coupled with the expenditure on his various ventures, had a serious effect on his finances. Parts of the estate were sold off in both 1911 and 1917, presumably to raise capital. Hugh died in 1943 and his wife and family then moved into Hunstrete Cottage, which was formerly the estate manager's house.

Eric Tremayne Buller Leyborne Popham (1894 - 1993)

Eric Tremayne Buller was born in 1894. He was the son of Elinor Louise and Arthur Tremayne Buller and a nephew of Sir Redvers Buller, who distinguished himself in the Boer war. He attended Harrow school and Oxford University, then followed an army career serving in the Duke of Cornwall's light infantry. Many people in his regiment were from his own estate of Downes near Tiverton. He married Dorothy Bridget Trywhitt Drake and they had three daughters.

He inherited Hunstrete in 1943 due to a financial arrangement made between his uncle and his mother and on doing so added her surname of Leyborne Popham to his. He subsequently moved to Hunstrete where the family lived for 13 years.

After the war he continued to serve in the army in both Gibraltar and India, attaining the rank of major before his retirement. He was a keen cricketer, being a member of Lords, and the game was played at Hunstrete on land that now belongs to the riding stables. There was a pavilion sited under the adjacent beech trees and locals can recall watching the matches that took place.

As the financial burden of running Hunstrete became increasingly onerous he finally took the decision to sell the remainder of the estate in 1956. It was split into numerous lots including the house itself, the four farms, the cottages, the woods and shooting rights and the agricultural land. The sale took place on 18th December, thereby ending an association of the Popham family with Hunstrete spanning three and a half centuries. He died in 1993 and is buried in Marksbury churchyard.

Water

The springs issuing forth from the surrounding hills have always provided Hunstrete with a ready source of water. The various occupiers of the site utilised this constant and plentiful supply in a variety of ways, both functional and ornamental, throughout the centuries. Initially influential in a choice of site for settlement, the streams would have been used for everyday domestic purposes.

In mediaeval times a stream was diverted to fill the moat surrounding the manor. The function of this was probably more decorative than defensive and would have been indicative of wealth and status. The same body of water was also used to supply the fishponds. It then flowed north east, sinking below ground beyond the village and re-emerging at Wick Farm, from whence it flowed into Compton Dando to join the River Chew.

A village pump is mentioned in 1705 and was likely to have been situated on, or near, the green. This would have been a more convenient form of water supply than springs and was probably installed in the late mediaeval period. Wells were also sunk with cottages either having their own, or access to one. An example of this is cottages 7 and 8 which both have a right of way to the well at number 6. Hunstrete House and Park Farm each had their own pump.

Another source was the stream that flows through Hunstrete Plantation. Water was taken from here and pumped back uphill, from where it was gravity fed to supply Hunstrete House and many of the properties on the estate. A hydraulic ram was built for this purpose, probably when the Grand Mansion was being constructed, and its remains can still be seen in the wood. When the Hunstrete Estate was disposed of in 1956, many of the properties were listed as being on estate water. Others had wells and or pumps, and some benefited from both, but all now receive their main supply from 'Bristol Water.' In keeping with the priorities of the day, Hunstrete House, Park Farm and even the cattle troughs in the fields were connected to mains water, in the middle of the 20th century, before the cottages in the village!

The pump in the farmyard, prior to the conversion of Barnwell

The well, still in existence, at number 6 Hunstrete

Fishponds

Sometime in the Middle Ages, probably contemporary with the acquisition of Hunstrete by Glastonbury Abbey, a chain of fishponds was constructed. Fish were an important source of food in mediaeval times both to religious communities and the secular population. Only the wealthier members of society owned fishponds and they often formed part of the manorial demesne. They were fed by springs or small streams and would be situated close to the manor house for both convenience and security.

The ponds were created by damming watercourses and if grouped together were controlled by sluices. They needed a constant supply of water running through, to provide the fish with oxygen, and a bypass system to draw off water in time of flood. There were two types with smaller, often very shallow, rectangular ones, called stews or store ponds, used for breeding or for holding fish for immediate consumption. Larger, deeper ones were also needed, to store fish for future use. These would often be small, needing to be fattened up until large enough to eat. Moats were also used for this purpose and this may have occurred at Hunstrete. The fish would be caught in rivers and transferred to the ponds, with typical specimens being trout, carp, tench and perch.

The fishponds at Hunstrete were originally a chain of five rectangular ones, situated a little distance to the north of the mediaeval manor. They are specifically referred to in a lease of 1755 and clearly marked on the estate map of 1759 (see page 6).

They were separated by stone walls, containing sluices, of which few traces now remain. A map of 1826 shows the line of a stream flowing from the fishponds to the Compton Dando road, just north of the village, where it sinks underground. The first pond is still intact and now forms an ornamental feature in the field belonging to The Chase.

Ornamental pond, once the first in a chain of five fishponds, at Hunstrete

A depression, which fills up with water in wet weather, marks the site of the second pond. Part of the outline of some of the others can be made out in a line to the north east, if one studies the topography closely. The path of the stream and most of the ponds were filled in during the last century. The Bath and North East Somerset Sites and Monuments Register records the following entry

> BN1288
>
> *Fishpond. Crawford notes a second fishpond to N of that published and infers it is medieval...There is a string of 3 dry fishponds CST64496244 all formed by pond bays which incorporate dry stone walling and are probably late medieval or later.*

The fishponds at Hunstrete follow the typical pattern of others in the surrounding area, according to Denison and Isles in an article on 'Mediaeval Fishponds in Avon', being rectangular, 75 - 100 metres long and 20 - 40 metres wide.

Hunstrete Lake

The main lake at Hunstrete looking west

The ornamental lake, formerly within the Hunstrete Estate, appears to have been constructed in the latter half of the 18th century. It was part of the landscaping for the Grand Mansion and was laid out so that it was overlooked from the front of the house, through stands of trees framing the view. This was very much in the 'natural' style of the day. Its designer cannot be identified but it is comparable to the work of Lancelot ' Capability' Brown and Humphry Repton. Each had been employed, at different times, to landscape Newton Park, the home of the Langtons, a short distance away. The Pophams may well have engaged one or other of these landscape architects, being keen follows of fashion, having seen the results of their handiwork whilst visiting their near neighbours.

The lake was constructed in an ideal situation where porous sandstone meets impervious clay. The lower lying land here would have been naturally boggy and the clay could be 'puddled' to make it watertight. This was usually achieved by walking oxen up and down the excavated bed, their feet treading it into a hardened layer. The lake has a depth of approximately four feet at the narrow end and 10 - 12 feet at the wider one. There is a dam at the shallow end, holding back a small body of water now known as Bridge Pool, which is enhanced by several ornamental arches.

An earth embankment, along its northern edge, retained the water in the lake itself. The outlet was formerly via a sluice supported by two large buttresses. The water escaped through a six inch diameter culvert, that may well have been used to pipe water from a spring to the mediaeval fishponds. The lake used to overflow regularly in winter and, when the dam burst in 1982, this sluice was removed and a new spillway constructed as part of the repairs. Also at this time a large bung was found in the bed of the lake. Any excess water flows into the fields and on towards Hunstrete Plantation. Here it joins the Candlestick Brook, from whence it flows into the River Chew at Woollard. There is a second flagstone lined culvert about two thirds of the way along the embankment.

The ornamental pool and bridge at Hunstrete c.1930

Until redesigned in the 1990's the lake had a withy bed at its western extremity, which may have been deliberately created when it silted up here. At the eastern end the small pool was converted into an ornamental pond, planted with water lilies, most likely in the early years of the 19th century. This is borne out by an entry in the account book for 1807 for the carriage of stones, lime and earth, for the pond wall and bank.

An ornate bridge was added around this time, surmounted by over 100 ornamental columns, as revealed in an account of 1806 which details payment for *stone balusters for the bridge*. Although the basic structure remains, little still exists of any decorative work. Plans to restore it, by Bathampton Angling Association, have been hampered by the lack of any evidence as to its original design. The balusters had been removed before the 1930's when the photograph (above) was taken.

As the uncompleted Grand Mansion deteriorated in the early 19th century so the lake suffered a similar fate from lack of maintenance. Skinner said in 1822

> *The noble piece of water is covered with weeds and long grass*

When the lake was cleared is uncertain but by the late 19th century it was restored to its former glory. During the early to mid 20th century it housed a collection of ornamental wildfowl and was used recreationally by the Leyborne Pophams for swimming, sailing and boating in the summer and ice skating in the winter, when conditions allowed. At this time the banks were open, with the trees which now line them having been planted some time after the mid 1940's.

Swimming at Hunstrete c.1934

Sailing at Hunstrete in the 1930's

In the early part of the 20th century the Leyborne Pophams allowed local villagers freedom to use the lake. Many older residents recall skating on the frozen water to the strains of music supplied by a wind up gramophone. Those who could not afford ice skates pulled each other along on kitchen chairs!

Boating at Hunstrete in the 1930's

Ice skating at Hunstrete in the 1930's

Swimming was also enjoyed, along with picnicking on the shore, until the drowning of an unfortunate local person on 12th July 1925. This led to it being, reluctantly, confined to family use. The local paper of the time recorded the following account

> *A Timsbury youth, George Henry Bowditch, aged 18 of Rose Cottages, Rectory Lane was drowned while bathing in the lake at Hunstrete. There were three other village youths with him at the time including Frank Church of Baker's Parade but none of them were apparently able to swim. There was a theory that he had got caught up in the weeds. The subsequent funeral service was held at the Congregational Church and was conducted by Rev. J. K. Bucknall.*

Fishing rights were granted to the Bathampton Angling Association in the early 1950's and remained in place when the estate was sold in 1956. This arrangement continued until they were able to purchase 10 acres of land, including the lake, in 1975. The total paid was £12,000 with part of this coming from a Sports Council grant. In 1987, with an eye to the future, they bought an adjacent area of some 11 acres of pasture, funded by a bank loan of £23,000. After much planning and consultation, including a dig by the Bath Archaeological Trust in 1996, the area was cleared for redevelopment (for further information see chapter on Archaeological Excavations).

This started in November 1997 with the aid of £5 000 from Bath & North East Somerset Council and a grant of £172 338 from the National Lottery. The original lake of five acres was retained, with two others being developed at the western and eastern ends. These are respectively the Withy Pool covering some three acres and the two and a half acre Bridge Pool, the spoil from which was used to create islands and to construct a large artificial mound that now prevents the lakes being viewed from Hunstrete House. It has been extensively planted with over 2 000 trees, along with other areas, to enhance the appearance of the site. A public footpath to Hunstrete Plantation skirts the north side of the main lake but the two pools have no general access.

The complex, known as The Hunstrete Fishery, includes 15 swims for the disabled, sponsored by Wessex Water, toilets and car parking. It reopened in March 1999 at a total cost of approximately £300 000. It was stocked with £30 000 of fish including bream, roach, tench, carp and barbel. The lakes, which are open all year, are a venue for both midweek and weekend match - fishing competitions. Catches include carp to 28lb, tench to 9lb, bream to 8½lb and pike to 20lb in the main lake with smaller fish in the pools. The largest fish ever caught was a 35lb mirror carp, taken from the main lake. In 1969 Hunstrete held the British eel record for a catch of an 8lb 10oz individual. This was stuffed and is on permanent display in Veal's fishing tackle shop in Bristol.

The lake supports a wide variety of wildlife particularly waterfowl. Coot, moorhen, mallard, great crested grebe and mute swan are all regular breeders. Tufted duck frequent the waters in winter and in March 1999 the very similar, but much rarer, ring necked duck from North America appeared with them for a few days. Cormorants often avail themselves of the free supply of fish, as do herons from time to time and the occasional kingfisher. On summer evenings Daubenton's bats can be seen feeding low over the surface of the water, alongside noctule bats patrolling the surrounding trees.

Toads used to breed in large numbers in the lake until the redevelopment in the 1990's. In early spring, on damp, rainy nights, hundreds would appear from the direction of Common Wood. As many were killed when crossing the road, a Toad Watch operated in the breeding season for some years. This comprised warning signs for traffic, together with a programme of assistance! A team of volunteers, the author included, collected the toads from the verges in buckets and carried them to the lake and safety. After the redevelopment of the lakes the numbers declined dramatically to single figures, never to recover, and the Toad Watch was eventually abandoned. However one traffic warning sign remains in place by the village green.

Ponds

The circular ornamental pond in the centre of the garden has been its focal point for several centuries. It appears on the 1759 map, but was probably added when later alterations were drawn, in the mid 1820's, as the ink appears to be a different colour. It lines up with both the central five arches of the Grand Mansion and the Hawhaw some distance to the north. This may be coincidental but is more likely to have been a deliberate element of garden design. The pond is about seven feet deep at the centre and about 30 feet in diameter. It contains some fine specimens of mature ornamental carp and a collection of water lilies.

There is a further rectangular pond to the west of the car park. This drains water from the roof of Hunstrete House. It was constructed in 1989 to supplement the water supply for the gardens, in times of drought. It is a haven for wildlife attracting water borne insects, frogs and dragonflies. Every year a pair of mallards bred on it and when their ducklings have hatched, the parents lead them through the grounds to the lake. It also supports a breeding pair of moorhens.

Woodland

The woodland surrounding Hunstrete has played an important role throughout its history. The first settlers in the area would have valued such a site with its ready supply of fuel and shelter from the worst of the elements. By the time of the Anglo Saxon Charter in AD936 a game enclosure had been established, in what was an eminently suitable habitat for such a venture.

The Domesday Book of 1086 records Marksbury as having 40 acres of woodland. This would have been a considerable amount since the large scale clearance of previous centuries. Woods are also listed in Glastonbury Abbey surveys of 1258, the early part of the 14th century and 1517. The latter alludes to a sylvan setting and specifically mentions extensive woodland at both Hunstrete and Marksbury.

It is likely that the area around Hunstrete has always been wooded. However since the early days of the estate it would have been managed, to a greater or lesser degree. Glastonbury Abbey certainly did so, deriving a considerable source of income from the timber. When the estate was returned to Henry VIII, after the suppression of the monasteries in 1539, the value of the woodland was estimated at well over £100 and the yearly income from this at 60 shillings.

The 1517 survey also refers to a common wood where all the tenants had rights, as was the practice under the mediaeval system of tenure. Called 'Lez Holte' and some 73 acres in extent, it is almost certainly what is known today as Common Wood. It was grazed by the cattle of the villeins of Marksbury and Hunstrete between 2nd February (Feast of the Purification) and the 2nd Tuesday after Easter (Hocktide). Thereafter it was reserved for the sheep flock of Wick Farm.

The Popham family carried on the programme of management when they acquired Hunstrete in the early years of the 17th century, as their accounts show. The earliest record is for 1649 - 1650 and refers to work in Ye Holt. This is obviously the same wood mentioned previously. In 1738 the following appears in the estate management records

> *Thomas Salmon of Marksbury - bond not to cut down Mr Edward Popham's timber.*

In 1786 there is a payment for cording 16 cord of wood. This was the practice of measuring felled wood, with one cord being 128 cubic feet. In November 1819 the accounts record a present of £1 to William Taylor for looking after Common Wood in nutting time, suggesting that the villagers no longer had rights there.

Samuel Braine was the woodsman in 1827, employed at a salary of £4 per year, and would have been responsible for all aspects of woodland management. In 1828 there is a payment to John Hopgood for cutting saplings, a practice carried out in managed woodland, to prevent them taking water and nutrients from the mature trees.

There are many records of replanting with the earliest being from 1713, when 239 beech trees were purchased at a cost of £16 16s 6d. They were brought by carriage from Gloucestershire, for planting in Houndstreet Park. These may well have been used to create the long avenue of trees shown on the 1759 estate map (see page 6).

Exploration of the area where these were broadly located has revealed the presence of a number of ancient beeches still remaining, in what is now Hunstrete Plantation. Although surrounded by other trees and undergrowth, it is still possible to pick out, what appears to be, the line of part of the avenue.

A list of the trees is provided by the survey accompanying the estate map of 1759, compiled by John Hinde. This records the following species:

In the vicinity of the house:
45 horse chestnut
50 sycamore
1 timber oak
3 timber ash
28 pollarded ash
1 timber elm

In the area of the bowling green and arch (now the car park):
9 timber oak
1 pollarded oak
2 pollarded ash
2 timber elm
3 maiden elm
2 pollarded elm

The schedule accompanying this map also refers to Witcomb Copse, which still exists as Whidcombe Brake, situated on the hill due south of Hunstrete House.

Subsequent to this a comprehensive timber valuation survey of 1775 recorded all the trees on the Hunstrete estate in the manors of Pensford, Publow and Woollard, Compton Dando, Hunstrete, Chelwood, Farmborough and Marksbury. Each tree was numbered, its type recorded e.g. maiden oak, the measurements of its length and girth taken and its timber content assessed. The total was 552 oak, 188 elm, 93 ash and 14 witch hazel (for further details of those recorded at Hunstrete see appendix 11).

The age and condition of these trees would have been of great importance, as the estate, under the Popham's ownership, was still actively engaged in timber production, both for its own use and as a trading commodity. Indeed they prosecuted anyone who was found to have tampered with any of the trees, including saplings (see chapter on Law and Order). The tree survey and notes in the account books illustrate their degree of involvement in the timber trade. In March 1772 Francis Stokes, a trustee, wrote

> *Attend Mr Poore and treating with him for sale of the timber in Houndstreet Park*

In January 1774 the following is recorded, which brings events vividly to life

> *Mr Stokes clerk's journey to Houndstreet, attendance of the surveyors and taking down the measure and value of the timber and assisting the surveyors out three weeks, and his expenses during that time, and to Mr Stokes journey selling the timber and breaking a confederacy formed by the Bristol people who wanted to buy it at under value by which means a competitorship was raised and the timber was sold for some hundreds above the value, travelling expenses and giving a dinner and liquor to the buyers according to custom   £47 9s 1d*

It seems likely that the survey, followed by the sale of the timber, took place in order to part finance the building of the Grand Mansion.

Other records show the purchase of various species of trees over a subsequent period. In 1792 there was a payment for 1 000 firs and 100 larches, followed by a further 960 larches in 1827. These coniferous species, known for their fast growing qualities, may have been used to provide shelter belts, tracts of woodland in which to rear game birds or for timber to supply pit props to the local mining industry. In 1805 records show that 12 elms were planted in the park and a further 11 dozen in 1814. Also mentioned are walnut, ash, oak and withies. The latter were probably used to create the withy bed at the western end of the lake, with a further purchase to the value of £100 occurring in 1818. They were grown in damp or boggy ground, harvested annually in rotation, and used to weave hurdles, baskets and so on.

In 1813 the estate woods are listed as:

> *A wood in Chelwood*
> *4 woods in Compton Dando*
> *Whitcombe Coppice in Marksbury*
> *Hoard Hill Coppice*
> *Naylor's Coppice*
> *Atgrove Wood on Wick Farm*
> *Modern plantation in Marksbury*
> *New plantation*
> *Garden orchard now in plantation*
> *Common Wood*

There is also a reference in the document to walnut timber and five acres of oak coppice. Coppicing is an ancient art where trees are regularly cut down to stools, or stumps, just above ground level. This practice encourages the production of small shoots, suitable for a number of purposes when harvested. In 1818 the estate purchased 100 pollarded ash trees at a cost of 8s 4d each. Pollarding was similar to coppicing with the trees being trimmed at the head, instead of the base.

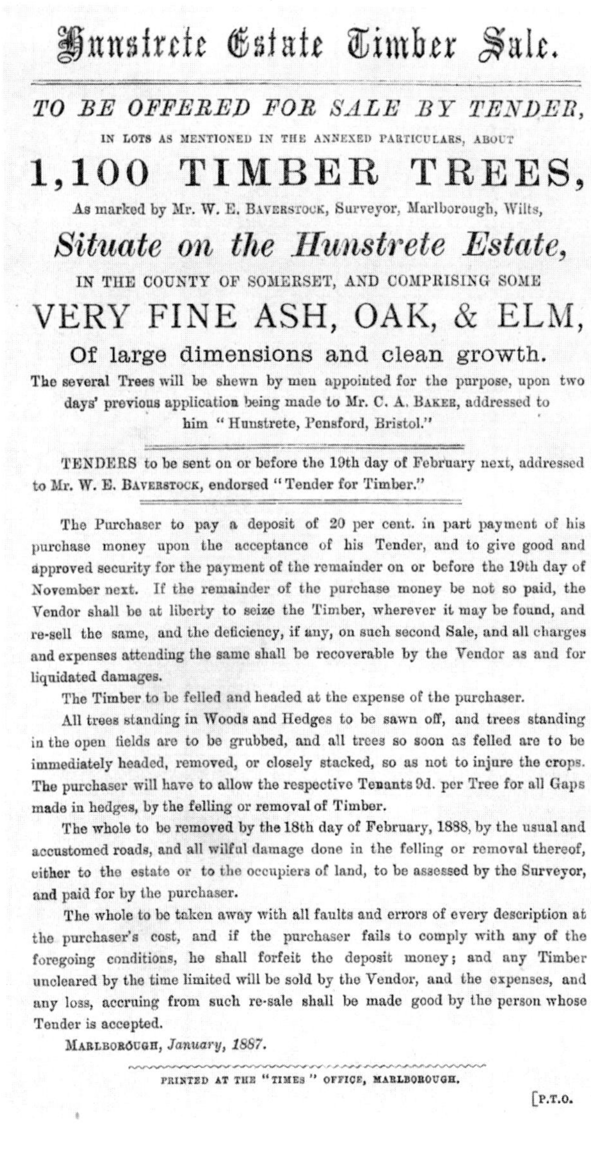

Hunstrete Estate Timber Sale.

TO BE OFFERED FOR SALE BY TENDER,

IN LOTS AS MENTIONED IN THE ANNEXED PARTICULARS, ABOUT

1,100 TIMBER TREES,

As marked by Mr. W. E. BAVERSTOCK, Surveyor, Marlborough, Wilts,

Situate on the Hunstrete Estate,

IN THE COUNTY OF SOMERSET, AND COMPRISING SOME

VERY FINE ASH, OAK, & ELM,

Of large dimensions and clean growth.

The several Trees will be shewn by men appointed for the purpose, upon two days' previous application being made to Mr. C. A. BAKER, addressed to him "Hunstrete, Pensford, Bristol."

TENDERS to be sent on or before the 19th day of February next, addressed to Mr. W. E. BAVERSTOCK, endorsed "Tender for Timber."

The Purchaser to pay a deposit of 20 per cent. in part payment of his purchase money upon the acceptance of his Tender, and to give good and approved security for the payment of the remainder on or before the 19th day of November next. If the remainder of the purchase money be not so paid, the Vendor shall be at liberty to seize the Timber, wherever it may be found, and re-sell the same, and the deficiency, if any, on such second Sale, and all charges and expenses attending the same shall be recoverable by the Vendor as and for liquidated damages.

The Timber to be felled and headed at the expense of the purchaser.

All trees standing in Woods and Hedges to be sawn off, and trees standing in the open fields are to be grubbed, and all trees so soon as felled are to be immediately headed, removed, or closely stacked, so as not to injure the crops. The purchaser will have to allow the respective Tenants 9d. per Tree for all Gaps made in hedges, by the felling or removal of Timber.

The whole to be removed by the 18th day of February, 1888, by the usual and accustomed roads, and all wilful damage done in the felling or removal thereof, either to the estate or to the occupiers of land, to be assessed by the Surveyor, and paid for by the purchaser.

The whole to be taken away with all faults and errors of every description at the purchaser's cost, and if the purchaser fails to comply with any of the foregoing conditions, he shall forfeit the deposit money; and any Timber uncleared by the time limited will be sold by the Vendor, and the expenses, and any loss, accruing from such re-sale shall be made good by the person whose Tender is accepted.

MARLBOROUGH, *January, 1887.*

PRINTED AT THE "TIMES" OFFICE, MARLBOROUGH.

[P.T.O.

Sale catalogue of timber from the Hunstrete estate in 1887

The Labour and Wages Book for 1883 - 84 reveals that Hunstrete Plantation was laid out at this time and that larch in Park Copse was felled. A catalogue for the sale of timber in 1887 is indicative of the scale of felling on the estate and reveals that trees were removed from Lord's Wood, Publow and Compton Dando including Pigsmoor Coppice, Park Coppice, Atgrove Coppice and land at Tucking Mill.

In 1905 the estate woods are listed as:

Hunstrete Plantation
Whidcombe Brake
Common Wood
Roundhill Wood
Fir Copse
Atgrove Wood

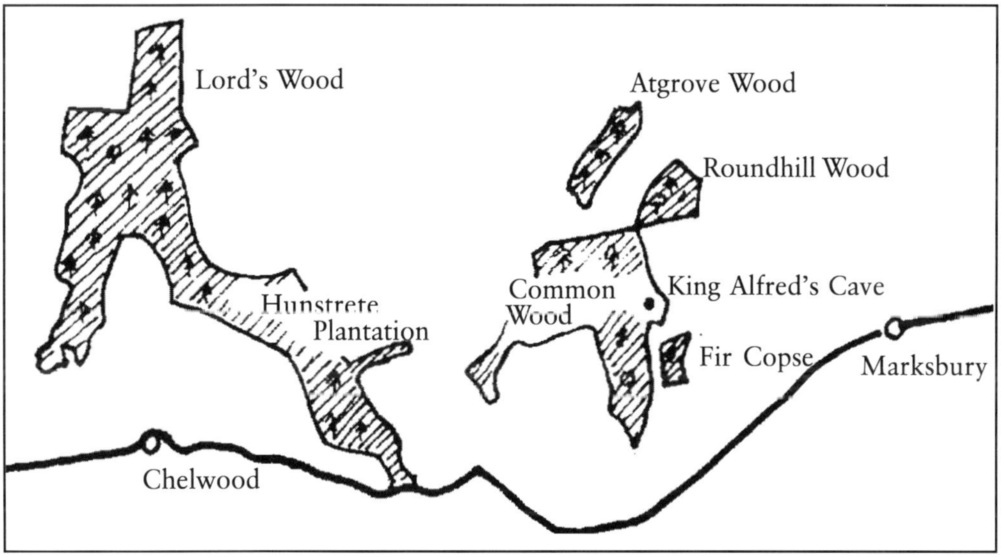

Hunstrete estate woods, Whidcombe Brake being to the south

In 1956 when the Hunstrete Estate was disposed of by the Popham family, 340 acres of wood were sold as a separate lot. Sir Christopher Chancellor, the subsequent owner, purchased Whidcombe Brake and Hunstrete Plantation. Atgrove Wood was included as part of Wick Farm, whilst Lord's Wood, Roundhill Wood, Fir Copse and Common Wood were sold to private purchasers. Parts of the latter are now used recreationally for pheasant shooting, archery and by Bristol Outdoor Pursuits Centre as a venue for paintballing. This is the practice of mock combat, with the participants shooting each other using coloured balls of paint, leaving a mark on the intended target, if successful.

Further stretches of woodland have continued to come on the market from time to time, most recently Whidcombe Brake, which was sold in 2003. When Hunstrete Plantation, which is currently up for sale, changes hands, the Hunstrete Estate will end its long and historic association with the production of timber.

There are a number of mature trees still standing in the grounds of the hotel including a line of ancient beech trees on top of the bank, overlooking the site of the Grand Mansion. It is possible that these were planted at the time of the landscaping surrounding the building in the late 18th century. In 1995 Arcadian Hotels commissioned a tree report prior to the construction of a leisure complex on the land that forms the car park. This concluded that a beech here was 158 - 200 years old, and another 126 years old, that a sweet chestnut was 204 years old and that an oak was 173 - 200 years old.

Horse chestnut tree, by the old entrance gate, planted to celebrate the birth of Elizabeth Leyborne Popham in 1909

The Park

The use of the word 'park' has changed considerably over time. The term was derived from the Old English word *pearroc* meaning an enclosed piece of land. In the Middle Ages it was used exclusively for a deer park but by the 18th century had come to mean a landscaped park. At Hunstrete, throughout the course of time, it was all three. By the 1720's a fashion had started for rolling parkland, clumps of trees and stretches of water, extending into the distance beyond a ha-ha. The landscape design of the 1770's encompassed all these features, most of which still remain, to a greater or lesser degree.

The park was originally some 3 000 acres in extent. I am uncertain how it was originally delineated but from at least the late 17th century, the edge was marked by a wall or by boundary markers. These were stones engraved with the initials of the various Popham owners. The one shown alongside is that of Dorothy Popham, wife of Sir Francis Popham who built the Grand Mansion. It was one of two found in Atgrove Wood. A later version bearing the initials of Edward William Leyborne Popham and dated 1841 is located in Compton Dando. About half of the land had been disposed of by the time of the 1956 sale. The remainder went as various lots with Hunstrete House retaining 90 acres.

The Deer Park

By the time of the Saxon Charter of AD936 the land surrounding Hunstrete was almost certainly an enclosed area used for the keeping of game, most probably deer, and remained so for several centuries thereafter. However the earliest reference to substantiate this only dates from 1705 when a note appears in the estate accounts saying

> *Paid for advice about ye deer killed out of the park.*

Mediaeval deer parks were used for farming venison to provide a ready supply of meat. They were enclosed by a substantial earth bank, surmounted by a deer proof palisade; comprising a ring fence of vertical stakes or pales. Hunting was ancillary taking place in the forest or chase, into which deer were released from the park.

Deer parks were known to have existed in late Saxon England, as at Hunstrete, but the Normans were the real innovators. Most monastic estates included a deer park and this may well be the reason why the Abbey of Glastonbury maintained an interest here. Parks varied in size but were at least 30 acres and normally between 100 and 200 acres. They were almost invariably in wooded country, again underlining the suitability of Hunstrete for this purpose.

Before the Conquest of 1066 there were only red and roe deer in Britain. The Normans introduced fallow deer and stocked them in the parks. This species is notoriously difficult to contain and many escaped into the surrounding countryside, where they quickly established breeding populations. None of this species now exists in the wild, in the area around Hunstrete. However there is a large population of our native roe deer and a small number of muntjac, another introduced species.

Emparkment required a costly Royal Licence and by the 13th and 14th centuries ownership had become a significant status symbol. The acquisition of this and the possession of resources necessary to maintain a park was considered to be an indication of considerable influence and privilege, as well as wealth.

Widespread decimation of the working population caused by the spread of the plague in the 14th century led to labour becoming expensive; consequently disparking took place on a large scale during the 15th to the 17th centuries. Only the wealthiest managed to maintain their parks, which included Hunstrete among their number.

How long the deer park continued to function is unclear. In 1818 there is a bill for two sacks of beans for the deer and in 1821 a payment for four men for catching a deer out of the park. From then on I can find no further references on the subject.

The Deer Herd

When the Dupays purchased the Hunstrete estate in the late 1970's they decided to restock the park. They initially installed four fallow deer that soon multiplied. The current herd comprises approximately 25 to 30 animals with one breeding buck, a young buck and the remainder does and fawns. The numbers are regulated by the amount of available grazing and the deer are culled annually.

They are fed daily at about 3.00pm with grass clippings, carrots, greens, potato peelings and bread and are given a supplement of sugar beet in winter. They also graze the grass within the park, which is fully enclosed by deer fencing. The trees in the deer park have a distinct browse line, at the height the animals can reach when standing on their hind legs.

They are a self-maintaining herd with the young being born about the middle of June. Two does regularly have twins and the rest single fawns. They are born in grass forms and can run around within hours. The rut, when the bucks fight for supremacy, takes place at the end of October. The dark winter coat starts to moult in April and the light spots are fully revealed about six weeks later. The males shed their antlers around May and these are collected and kept.

Fallow deer herd in the park at Hunstrete in the 1980's

Rabbits

Initially, besides deer, the park was used for the keeping of rabbits. These were introduced into Britain by the Normans and kept in specially constructed warrens, maintained by a warrener, as a ready supply of food. In 1754 a document refers to Thomas Allwood as warrener and gamekeeper. The tithe map of 1843 has a warrener's cottage specifically identified on it, deep in Hunstrete Plantation and fields to the east of this called Upper and Lower Warren.

In 1806 a survey and valuation of the manor recommended that the warren be discontinued as the rabbits were impoverishing the grazing for the deer and that the park be stocked with cattle such as Scotch or Welsh bullocks and sheep. This appears to have been implemented, as a payment of £69 10s 0d *to James Fisher for 3 score Welsh weather sheep* is shown in the accounts of 1810.

The Park Wall

When the wall surrounding the park was built has been impossible to establish. The first evidence comes from an account book of 1705 when payments were made to two masons for mending the breaches in the park wall and for six new gateposts for the park. This indicates it must have been built some years earlier to be in need of repair. Subsequent entries detail continuing restoration and further construction._To maintain it effectively must have placed an enormous strain on the estate's resources. Shown are just a few of the bills, which apply to the wall, out of numerous examples:

1777	*58 days work by up to four men on the park wall*	
1806	*Hewing and morticing 90 park posts*	
1822	*By Robert Ford and Richard Poole for building 100 perch of wall in the park 4½ feet high at 2s per perch*	*£18 0s 0d*
1826	*By Robert Ford for building 500 perch of wall at 6d per perch*	*£12 0s 0d*
1827	*By Robert Ford for building 539 perch of wall in the park at 6d per perch*	*£13 9s 0d*
1830	*Robert Ford for repairing Park wall*	

Although the wall has long since fallen into disrepair, parts of it, and an indication of the distance it covered, can be found by following public footpaths. Initially alongside Hunstrete Lake to its farthest point and then into the trees. As you enter Hunstrete Plantation turn to the right and follow the track that skirts the boundary. The remains of the wall are to your right.

The remains of the park boundary wall in Hunstrete Plantation with ancient coppice behind

Hedging and Ditching

Hedging and ditching also took place regularly in the park as the following records from the account book show

1790 Purchase of 22 250 thorn plants

1819 120 lug open trenching

1822 Wm Prior 30 lug of hedge

1825 James Clement for making a hedge 31½ lug and planting the same in the park at 9d per lug

James Clement for digging a ditch and making a double hedge

1826 Purchase of 10 000 thorn plants

The hedges would have been to control stock. The ditches were also for this purpose and to aid drainage. There are also payments for the digging of drains to supplement that provided by the ditches. In 1832 the accounts show 241 lug of stone draining was laid in the park and 27 lug in Redfield.

Trees

Additional trees were planted in the Park both for timber and as ornamentation. The 1759 estate map (see page 6) shows avenues of trees leading up to the mediaeval manor house and what I assume to be a lodge. The later alterations on this map also show four clumps of trees around the lake, that were obviously planted to enhance its setting. Various records exist for the planting of trees in the park including 18 evergreens in 1826 and larch and oak in 1831.

Lodges

The records show that there were several lodges and lodge houses at Hunstrete, particularly in mediaeval times. The 1644 inventory refers to the Porter's lodge and the 1759 map shows a range of buildings surrounding the manor itself, some of which would have been for this purpose. The new lodge referred to in the late 17th century may well be the separate building to the north west of the main complex. The building that forms the core of the present Hunstrete House was referred to as the Lodge at the beginning of the 19th century and was apparently used to house the Popham family and their guests, when they travelled from Littlecote to Hunstrete for the shooting.

The Ice House

Icehouses were introduced to Britain from France during the 17th century. From then until the 19th century they were located in the parks of great houses. The example at Hunstrete is most likely to have been contemporary with the construction of the Grand Mansion. An artificial earth mound concealed a domed or barrel vaulted roof, with a stone or brick walled chamber, an egg shaped ice well, a narrow entrance tunnel and doors designed to maintain an even temperature within. Melted ice discharged via a drain in the base of the ice well, in which a grill covered with reeds or straw, protected an air trap. The principal was the same as that of an 'S' bend in a sink.

The mound had an impervious clay cap beneath a covering of soil or turf, as damp could ruin the contents within. It was built in an open elevated position to aid rapid evaporation and the dispersal of rainwater. Ice houses were situated near a lake from which ice was removed in winter, crushed and then compressed in the ice well to form a solid mass. This was shovelled in at the top and removed when necessary via the narrow tunnel.

They often had a building attached in which perishable food could be stored, as does the Hunstrete example. This was destroyed in January 1990 when a beech tree fell onto it during a storm and was restored a year later. It is a grade II listed building (for entry see appendix 8). Although the listing dates it as mid 19th century I believe it is more likely to be late 18th century.

Entrances

There have been a number of entrances to Hunstrete House over the centuries, from a variety of directions. The present drive was created in 1986 when the house was first converted to a hotel. A condition of planning permission being granted was that the use of the entrance from the A368 was considered too dangerous and a new one had to be created from the minor road to the east.

A white gate on the major road, from which an imposing view of the house can be had, marks the former entrance. Adjacent to this is a horse chestnut tree planted in 1907 to mark the birth of Elizabeth, Hugh and Janet Leyborne Popham's eldest daughter (see page 64). The drive was lined by elm trees, some of which remain and indicate the line it took. Previous to this the front drive deviated slightly, terminating at the former main entrance on the west side of the house.

The route to the house from the Compton Dando road, past the lake, was always known as the back entrance but has become disused in recent years.

The Grand Mansion was approached from the Hunstrete to Compton Dando road via an imposing drive of crushed red marl, the remains of which were uncovered during archaeological excavations in 1990. It swept in a large curve up to the house where it culminated in a circular terminus, adjacent to which was a large portico. The remains of this now form the five arches. In the centre of the terminus was what looks like a shrub border on the 1806 map (see page 7).

The approaches to the mediaeval manor are uncertain. One is likely to have followed the line of the public footpath that skirts the lake before entering Hunstrete Plantation. Others were probably that marked by the long avenue of trees shown on the 1759 estate map and one from the lodge to the north west (see page 6).

A bill of 1829 details payment for four new iron gates but where these were is uncertain.

The Swimming Pool

This was built in the 1980's when Hunstrete House became a hotel. It occupies the site of what used to be the rhubarb patch and an area of rough grass. The changing rooms were designed to blend sympathetically with the other buildings in the grounds.

The Hunstrete Stables

These were formerly a stable and pigsties and are on the 1825 estate map. Berkshire pigs were kept during the first half of the 20th century and supplied meat for the house. In the time of the Dupays, a flock of about 100 Maran hens were housed here, their dark brown eggs supplying the hotel. The stables were considerably extended in 2001 and now house the award winning Haflinger horses of the Glyn Eryr stud. This was founded in 1989 and is owned by Major and Mrs R. Gillis. The breed comes from the mountains of the Austrian Tyrol where they were used as work animals.

The Park Stables

The estate accounts show that a barn and stables were built in the park in 1824 at a cost of £50 0s 0d. This may well have been following the recommendation of the 1807 survey (see appendix 12). The land on they stand no longer belongs to the estate and both form part of the private stables opened in 1990.

The Five Arches

The five arches are all that remain of the former Grand Mansion. They overlooked the lake before the Hunstrete fishing complex was developed and were left standing, as a romantic ruin, when the building was demolished in the 1830's. Built of rubble faced with Bathstone, they formed the front portico of a building that was 17 bays wide, giving an idea of the overall scale. In very dry summers the foundations of the building show and the five arches can be used as a reference point from which to trace the outline.

The five arches in the former park of the Hunstrete estate

The Hawhaw

This lies to the north of Hunstrete lake on land that formerly belonged to the estate. It is marked on the ordnance survey map and appears on the Bath and North East Somerset Sites and Monuments Register. It is a perfectly circular raised mound some 40 feet in diameter. Its purpose has provoked much speculation being variously described as a garden feature, a folly and a horse training ground.

Having studied it extensively on the ground I spent a considerable amount of time looking at various maps and reached no definite conclusion until I realised the following. The Hawhaw, the five arches and the circular pond in the centre of the gardens all, more or less, line up. This is no longer apparent on the ground due to alterations in the topography of the area, caused by redevelopment of the lakes. I have therefore concluded that the Hawhaw was most likely built as a garden feature for the Grand Mansion. As such it probably had, or was intended to have, a building on it, most likely a folly or gazebo.

Recreation in the Park

The park was used for a large number of events during the first half of the 20th century. These included cattle and dog shows, fetes, scout and guide camps, hunt meets and cricket matches. The latter were held in the field known as Pleasure Ground with a cricket pavilion situated below the line of beech trees at its southern edge. This was later moved to the area of trees beyond the croquet lawn.

The Gardens

Although there were probably gardens at Hunstrete from its earliest beginnings, no evidence can be found of these. They would have been those belonging to the people on site, who managed the deer herd, and would have been functional, providing food, rather than ornamental. The first documentary evidence of any form of garden is found in a charter of 1252. This confirms the gift by William Comyn, to his son John, of his estate at Hundestert and refers to the buildings together with gardens. These are again mentioned in 1305 when John grants it to Nicholas de Chiltenham. The next proof of their existence is to be found in the 1517 Glastonbury Abbey survey where both gardens and orchards are recorded. This is consistent with research on mediaeval gardens, which has established that there were various types:

A small ornamental garden, of under an acre, known as a herber. This was dominated by a lawn, sometimes with a fountain at its centre. It would be square in shape and edged with herbaceous borders containing ornamental flowers and aromatic herbs. There would be seating at the edges with vines and trees for shade.

An orchard of one to four or more acres laid out in a regular manner. This would have contained fruit and nut trees such as apples, pears, mulberries, cherries, plums, figs, nuts, almonds and quinces. It would be surrounded by a boundary of one sort or another: a hedge and ditch, a fence, a moat, or even a combination of these. Orchards were valued both for their crops and for the pleasure afforded by blossom, scent and shade.

The kitchen, or utilitarian garden, which was purely functional. It contained food and medicinal plants as well as those grown for strewing on floors, quelling insects, scenting water for washing and other household purposes. It also served as a market garden with any surplus produce being sold at recognised sites.

The little park or pleasure park as distinct from a hunting park. This was a miniature form of the latter and was preferably walled. It would have been planted with trees and bushes and supplied with a source of water to attract a wide variety of wild animals and birds. These were watched purely for pleasure with persecution being banned.

These types related to different social levels. Royalty and the nobility would have had all four gardens covering upwards of 15 acres. Such properties in England were commonly interwoven with moats and chains of ponds and lay adjacent to a large hunting park of some 200 acres. Owners of more moderate means would lay out the first three types only, over some two to five acres, perhaps enlarging the customary boundary ditches to make a prestigious moat.

Hunstrete in 1517, being two acres in extent, appears to fall into the second category, although the existence of a moat would have improved its social status. Archaeological excavations in 1994, prior to the lake being extended, revealed traces of gardens to the north and east of the manor complex. These included cobbled surfaces, paths, terraces, outlines of planting beds and part of the moat.

With the acquisition of the estate by the Popham family, in the early 17th century, changes inevitably occurred. A document of 1673 records rent for the glass houses of £20 0s 0d although no information can be found as to their location and usage. A lease of 1702 is the next document containing a specific reference mentioning *My Ladys Gardens* and *The Kitchen Garden* confirming that both pleasure and functional gardens still existed. Likewise a bill for pruning apple trees at Houndstreet in 1706 also proves the continued cultivation of orchards.

The 1759 map (see page 6) by John Hinde is the first pictorial representation of any form of garden plan. However, as this appears to have been used as the basis for later alterations to the estate, it is difficult to establish what the true layout was. The accompanying schedule specifically mentions *a bowling green and arch* located approximately at the far end of the present car park. This was an invariable feature of a Queen Anne garden and shows that the Pophams were following the fashion of the time. It was strongly advocated by J. J. James in 'The Theory and Practice of Gardening' in 1712

> *A Bowling Green is one of the most agreeable Compartments of A Garden, and, when 'tis rightly placed, nothing is more pleasant to the Eye. It's hollow Figure covered with a beautiful Carpet of Turf very Smooth, and of lively green, most commonly encompassed with a Row of tall Trees with Flower bearing shrubs, make a delightful composition, besides the Pleasure it affords us, of lying along its sloping Banks, in the shade, during the hottest weather.*

Other references to the garden are for the purchase of specific items, that give us tantalising glimpses into what it might have been like. A few of them are listed here:

1786	*Bill for plaster laths for the green house*
1788	*Glazier's bill for melon frames*
1790	*Purchase of garden pots*
	Bill for cucumber glass, mellon frames and green house
1793	*Glass for cucumber frames*
1806	*Payment for garden seeds*
1809	*Payment for garden seeds sent to St John's, Newfoundland*
1818	*Miller and Sweet's bill for seeds*

1820 Miller and Sweet's account for trees supplied
1823 Two bills each for 40 apple trees
1824 Purchase of 70 apple trees
1825 Bill for the grafting of apple trees

The latter payments must have been for the establishment of a new orchard as a document of 1828 refers to this by name. The remnants of these probably form the existing orchard to the west of the present gardens.

Maps of c. 1825 show the same layout as the 1759 plan with another smaller garden, arranged in a cross formation, to the west of the current house on what is now the croquet lawn.

By 1882 the Ordnance Survey map shows this has disappeared and the area is planted with trees. The large garden remains in similar format but again is shown as mainly tree covered, with the pond being the central feature (see page 8).

Apple picking in the orchard c.1934

The present walled garden appears to be late 18th century and may well have been laid out as part of the landscaping of the Grand Mansion. The gardener's store seems to have been built at the same time as the wall, and is incorporated into it. It appears to be about 200 years old being shown on the 1825 estate map and is a small one up, one down, structure that has the typically small paned Popham windows. A bill of 1787 *for glazing the hutt in the park* is likely to be for this building. Its original purpose is unclear but it may have been accommodation for estate staff, probably gardeners, or a garden store.

By the 1930's much of the garden had been turned over to orchards where prize-winning poultry were housed. There were also extensive rose gardens and pinks were cultivated. The head gardener at this time was Jesse Palmer. Several metal plant labels have recently been unearthed for both fruit and roses. These are as follows:

Apples: *King's Acre Pippin, Quarrenden Red, Coronation and Allington Pippin*

Pear: *Pitmaston Duchess*

Roses: *Tea Roses, Marie van Houtte and Comte de Raimbaud Hybrid Perpetual, Francois Michelor*

Apple and pear labels

Rose labels

Jesse Palmer c.1938

In 1806 the accounts show that the hill against the south front was levelled, presumably to improve the view. Photographs taken at the beginning of the 20th century show three circular flowerbeds at the front of Hunstrete House. The lawn outside the bar was used for tennis and croquet in summer. When the Dupays converted the house to a hotel a permanent tennis court was built to the north of the swimming pool. The same lawn is still used for croquet.

Views of the gardens in 1909 (left) and in the 1940's (right) with Ernest Barnes and Gillian among the herbaceous borders

Ernest Barnes, formerly of Compton Dando, was Head Gardener at Hunstrete in the 1940's and lived with his family in the gardener's cottage. This was situated in the block across the courtyard from the main house. His daughter Gillian recalls there being grass paths dividing up the main garden, as at present. She told me that these were flanked by beautiful herbaceous borders.

Over the course of the next few decades the gardens gradually declined, probably due to rising costs together with a lack of available labour. In the 1980's Mr Dupays decided to restore the gardens to their former glory. Assisted by a head gardener and three under gardeners, he cleared and replanted them, reproducing the original design. The dilapidated greenhouses were also renovated and pipistrelle bats now roost in the rear walls and can be seen flying around the gardens at dusk.

At this time there were extensive vegetable gardens, occupying most of the land to the east of the tennis courts, as far as the ice house. These supplied the hotel with fresh produce, as did the large area under fruit. This included blackcurrrants, redcurrants, whitecurrants, summer and autumn raspberries, loganberries, tayberries, Japanese wineberries and kiwi fruit. There were strawberry beds situated outside the staff quarters but these had to be moved to a less obvious location, as the produce proved too tempting to passers by! The gardens also provided cut flowers for the house.

However with changes of ownership the gardens once again deteriorated. Eventually a programme of restoration, planned by local horticulturist Mary Payne, was put in place in September 2001. The biggest problem was the widespread colonisation of many of the beds by ground elder and bindweed. A programme of spraying with glyphosate was instigated with everything in infested borders, however des-irable, being killed off to prevent these pernicious weeds being transferred to other areas. This started with the long borders leading to the swimming pool. They were replanted a year later with hot colour plants in the upper pair, nearest the croquet lawn and cool shades in the lower pair.

In spring 2000 the borders at the front of the house were cleared and replanted following a pink, purple, and silver theme. The transverse borders in the walled garden were also replanted at that time. In the following spring the large fruit cage was cleared and the area grassed over to reduce maintenance demands. A small amount of fruit for the

The ornamental pond and restored greenhouses

kitchen was replanted elsewhere. There is also a large vegetable garden that provides fresh seasonal produce for the hotel. The bed bordering the croquet lawn was sprayed in summer 2003 and was replanted in autumn of that year.

The renovation has followed a similar theme to that of Mr Dupays although the number of beds cultivated has had to be reduced. This is in order to make the gardens more manageable, as staff levels have fallen in recent years.

There is still an orchard to the rear of the kitchen containing the following trees: apple, pear, plum, walnut, medlar and black mulberry. These were all planted in the 1980's, apart from the plums. A few ageing apple and pear trees are all that remains of the orchard to the west of the walled garden of which one pear is over 65 years old. The fruit in both areas is not harvested but provides a valuable food resource for the local wildlife. There are also wild flower meadows beyond the croquet lawn.

Part of the ornamental fountain

The statues and ornamental pots, placed throughout the gardens, were sourced by Mrs Dupays, either from Italy or from antique shops. The figure at the end of the walled garden borders, the cherubs outside the entrance to Robin and the ornamental basin presently adjacent to the gardeners' store, all formed part of an ornate fountain. This was imported from Italy and was placed by Mrs Dupays as the central feature of the courtyard garden. Unfortunately it was shattered by frost, sometime after they sold the hotel, and had to be removed.

Hunstrete Village

That there has been some form of settlement at Hunstrete for hundreds of years is clear. However the first evidence as to the specific location of the actual village, its shape and size comes from a map drawn by John Hinde in 1759 (see page 6). This shows the present road through the village and a back lane running down the side of properties 10 and 11, behind 6, 7 and 8 and re-emerging at the rear of Hunstrete Cottage. This in effect formed an island on which were several houses and is still in existence on the 1806 estate map (see page 7). By 1846, when the tithe map was produced, it had disappeared with the former island bisected by the lane running along the rear of numbers 6, 7 and 8.

Aerial photograph of Hunstrete around the late 1970's

A 1 Hunstrete	F 5 Hunstrete	K 10 and 11 Hunstrete
B Hunstrete Cottage	G 6 Hunstrete	L Former Sawmills
C 2 Hunstrete	H 7 Hunstrete	M Barnwell
D Deacon's Yard	I 8 Hunstrete	N Park Farm
E 3 and 4 Hunstrete	J 9 Hunstrete	O Outbuildings of Park Farm

The 1759 map, apart from the manor complex, shows a total of 16 houses in the village. This is as far as can be deciphered, although as the actual document is very faint there may be more These occupy the approximate area of the present village, although the layout is somewhat different. There are also two houses in the woods. The accompanying schedule gives the names of the occupiers (see chapter on The People of Hunstrete).

In the 1780's Edmund Rack was collecting information for Collinson's 'History and Antiquities Of The County of Somerset'. His notes on Marksbury and Hunstrete still survive and state

> *It is a mean village, but pleasantly situated consisting of 54 houses, mostly thatch, 20 of which are in Hunstreet, a small hamlet and tything belonging this parish at which the late Francis Popham Es has began to build a large and elegant House, which is not yet finished.*

In 1813 documentary evidence reveals a new farmhouse was constructed, which I assume to be the present Park Farm. Interestingly it is the only property in the village to have a slate roof and was probably never thatched. It occupies the site of the former farmhouse and may well have been built on the same foundations. Similarly, materials may well have been reused. This is particularly so if one takes into account a lease of 1806 which refers to *a good farmhouse, stone and slate*, in the occupancy of Samuel Boulter, the same tenant as in 1759.

In the 19th century the number of households as shown by the census returns are as follows:

1841	10	9 buildings (probably 10 and 11 being divided in two) with at least 7 demolished
1851	13	of which 1 uninhabited (probably both 6 and 7 and 10 and 11 being divided in two)
1861	12	
1871	12	
1881	12	of which 2 uninhabited
1891	13	
1901	12	of which 1 uninhabited

This data shows that between 1841 to 1851 there were three additional properties. These were the newly built 3 and 4 Hunstrete, erected between 1844 and 1851, as they do not appear on the 1843 tithe map, and the division of 6 and 7. It seems from the fluctuation between 12 and 13 properties that this house has been divided and reinstated more than once.

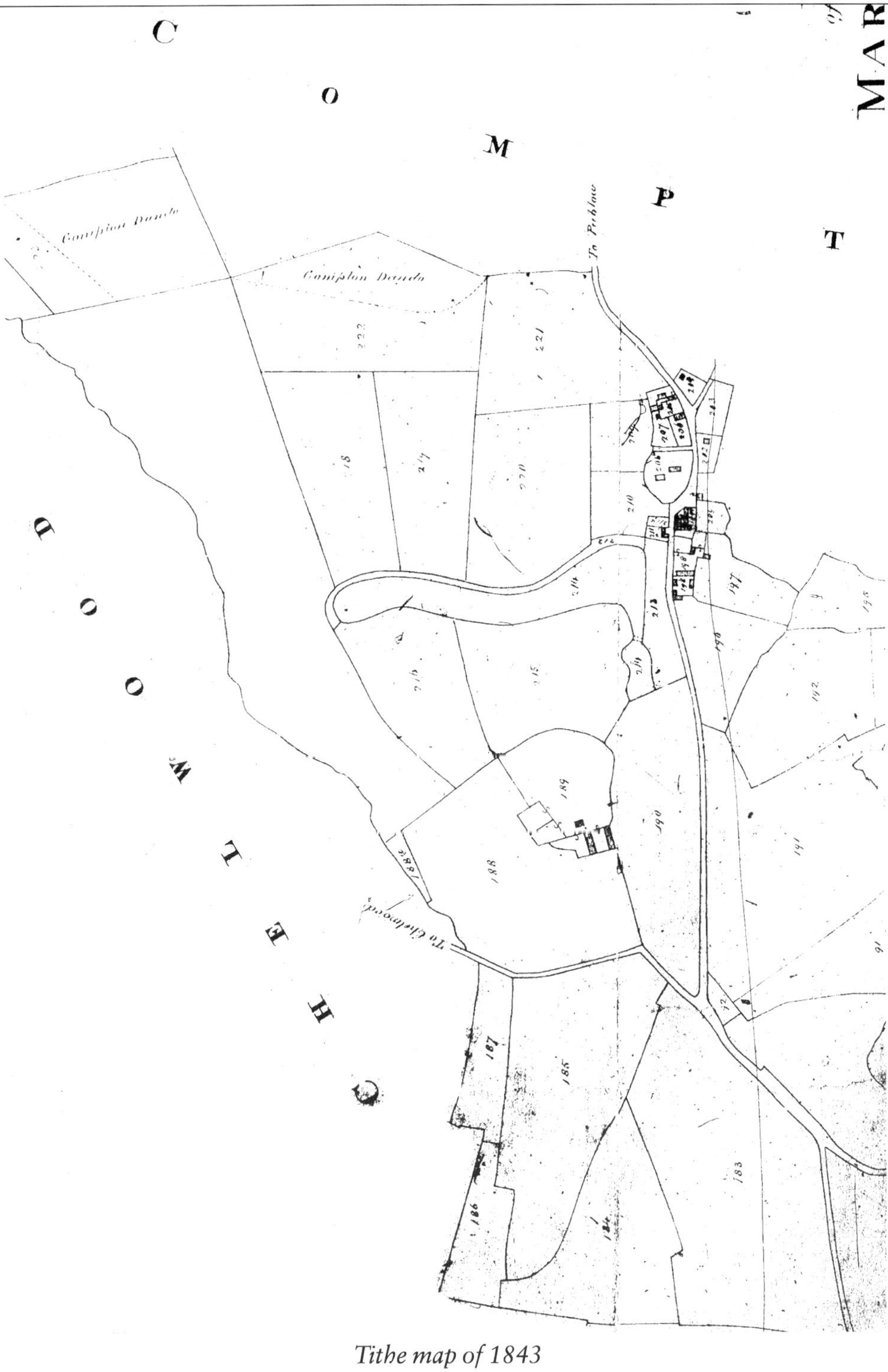

Tithe map of 1843

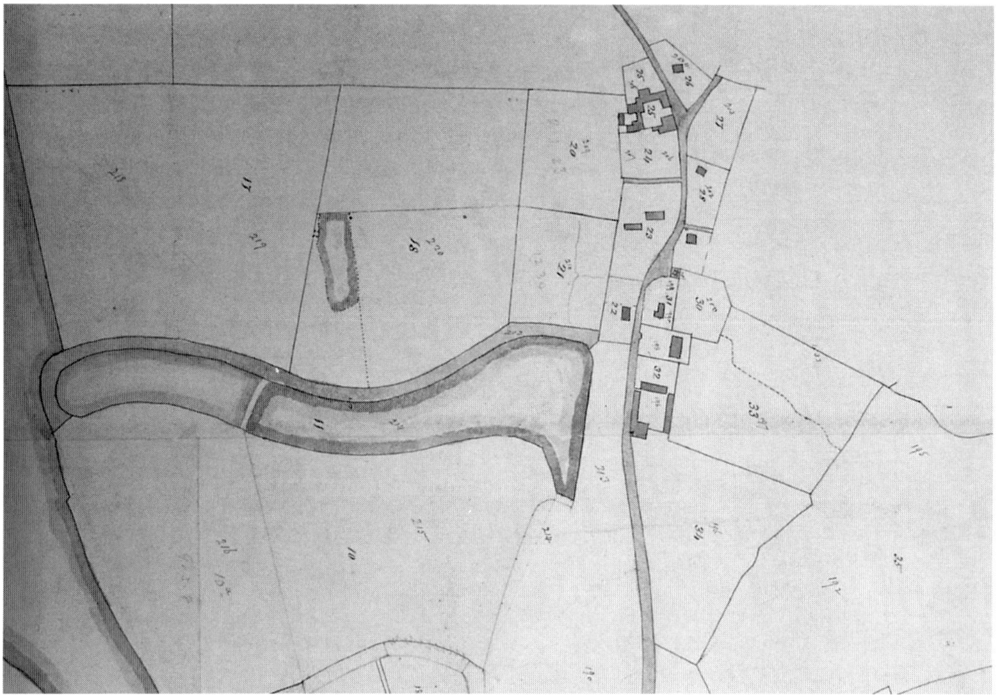

1866 Map of Hunstrete Village

In 1956 when the estate passed out of the hands of the Popham family the village comprised 12 cottages, together with a farm, a sawmill and a builder's yard. These were mainly two or three bedroomed properties with a living room, kitchen and scullery. Some had a separate wash house with copper, whilst others had these facilities as an integral feature. They had metal framed casement windows with small panes and ornate catches, identifying them as Popham properties, as did the initials EWLP or FWLP cut into interior woodwork such as door frames.

The buildings were of local stone probably from the quarry at Clayley, some mile or so distant. The roofs were pantiled, apart from one of slate, although most had formerly been thatched. Heating was by coal fires with cooking being done on a range. Mains electricity was connected in the 1950's. Water was formerly supplied by wells or the village pump and latterly by the Hunstrete estate, although some houses remained on their own supplies.

In the main, sanitation consisted of outside earth closets. There were large productive kitchen gardens, the fertility of which was no doubt aided by the contents of these being used on them. Each house was identified by its estate number, displayed as white lettering on a dark blue plaque, above the front door.

In the year 2003 the village is made up of 24 houses of which 14 are renovated older properties, mostly greatly extended, 9 are conversions of farm or other estate buildings and one is a new build. The houses are described in order as you enter the village from the Compton Dando direction. The details including the 1956 sale catalogue entries, which are quoted verbatim, are as follows:

Number 1 Hunstrete in the mid 1970's prior to alteration

Number 1

This is the first house on the left as you enter the village from the Compton Dando direction and was originally a small detached cottage. It was a tied cottage for the workers of Park Farm during the first half of the 20th century.

The 1956 estate sale catalogue entry is as follows:

> *Built of stone with a pan tiled roof. It contains:*
> *Sitting Room with fireplace, Kitchen with sink, range and copper, Scullery with cupboards and three Bedrooms, two with fireplaces and one being a landing bedroom. Outside: E.C.Pigsty, Good Garden, Mains Electricity and Well Water.*

In 1975 it was sold for £17 000 to owners who added a downstairs room to the right, an attached garage to the left, blocking up a window in the process, and

extended the scullery. In 1981 it was bought by its present occupants, who built an upper floor extension, creating three full sized bedrooms in the process. It also gave the cottage a more balanced appearance.

An odd large slab of stone lies in the hedge, that forms the boundary with the road, its original function unclear. Lots of pieces of china have been found in the garden together with the remains of clay pipes, most likely from an old rubbish dump in the days prior to waste collection.

Number 2 - Well House

This property is the first house on the right from the Compton Dando direction and is mostly hidden from view. The original front door faced the road with the property being accessed through the former Builder's Yard. This has since been altered, with it now being approached via a short drive.

Number 2 Hunstrete, gable end, and the courtyard viewed from the west

The 1956 estate catalogue entry is as follows:

> *It is built of stone with a pantiled roof and contains:*
> *Entrance porch. Sitting Room with modern tiled fireplace. Larder. Scullery with sink (hot and cold) and copper, Kitchen with 'Yorkist' combination stove with hot water boiler and heated airing cupboard. Bathroom with panelled bath (hot and cold) separate WC with low level WC suite, and Three bedrooms, two with fireplaces.*
> *Mains electricity. Estate Water. Septic Tank Drainage.*

The house is now a T shape with the cross bar being the original and the upright a conversion of an outbuilding that was attached to the house. Under the living room and hall are the cobbles that formed the floor of the barn. A fourth bedroom and second bathroom, together with a large stairwell are recent additions. The childrens' playroom was a single storey animal shelter.

Dipping in graphite has preserved the very large original door keys. Pieces of crockery and glass have been found in the garden, which also contains a well. The building takes its name from this, now being known as Well House.

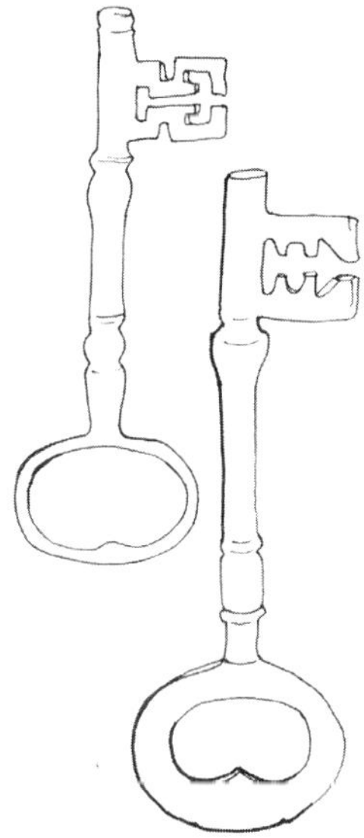

Original front door keys of 2 Hunstrete

The Estate Builder's Yard

The 1956 estate sale catalogue describes this complex as follows:

> *Grouped around the Estate Builder's Yard are a stone and tiled Paint Shop or Store Room with Store over, lean - to Blacksmith's Shop and two Builder's Stores, a stone and pantiled Garage and Store Room, and adjoining Wood and Fuel Store. Off the roadside are stone and tiled Wagon Shed and lean - to timber Carriage House. Other Buildings off the north drive include Lime House, Cider House, Loose Box, lean - to Coal Store, stone and pantiled Four - Stall Stable with Loft over and Concrete Yard.*
> *There is a productive Kitchen Garden on the north side of this lot.*
> *Hunstrete Water Supply.*

The outbuildings of the estate builders' yard have now been converted into houses.

The Gables

In the late 1990's the cartshed, or latterly boatshed, became a house known as The Gables. When shoots took place on the estate in the 19th century, the visiting coaches were housed here, with the stables being at Well House. The footmen and coach driver were billeted in Hunstrete Cottage, which was referred to as the 'Shooting Box.' In about 1980 an organ, bearing the date 1850, was found in the cartshed and may possibly have come from Hunstrete House. It is now in private ownership.

Deacon's Yard

Similarly in 2000 the estate builder's workshop was renovated and became Deacon's Yard. This was named after the Deacon family who worked for the estate for many years and bought the yard in the 1956 sale. They ran a building business from here. This is now let to tenants.

Hunstrete Cottage

This large house is on the right with its front door opening directly onto the road. It was formerly the home of the estate land agent for about two hundred years. When Hugh Leyborne Popham died in 1943 and the Bullers inherited, his wife, daughter Mary and infant granddaughter Beatrice, moved into here. They left in 1946 and for many years the house was rented. Since 1979 it has been lived in by Beatrice and her husband Richard, thereby maintaining the Popham link with the village. It was not included in the 1956 sale.

It has obviously been extended in the past, having five bedrooms, four of which are large doubles. The southern aspect is thought to be the oldest part. There are several bills for valuing the work of the steward's house in 1816 so this may well be when major alterations occurred. The house has slate floors at ground level. There used to be a doorway in the middle and it may have been two cottages at one time. Outside are two back to back privies, which would seem to substantiate this.

Beatrice remembers as a child, there was a long straight shelf in the room next to the dairy, where bowls of junket were left to set. Above this was a pigeon loft and below cellars. She also recalls the estate workers collecting their wages from the 'Gun Room' at Hunstrete Cottage where the estate guns were then stored.

At the rear of the property was a small courtyard containing a cartshed and a two storey stable. The latter housed the generator, this being on the ground floor, prior to mains electricity coming to the village.

The Courtyard

In the 1980's the cartshed, garage and potting shed of Hunstrete Cottage were converted into a dwelling known as The Courtyard. This is now let.

Number 3

This is a semi-detached cottage and is the most northerly of a pair with number four, situated on the east side of the road through the village.

The 1956 sale catalogue entry is as follows:

> *Built of stone with a tiled roof and has metal framed casement windows.*
> *Comprises:*
> *Entrance Porch, Sitting Room with tiled fireplace. Living room with range and cupboards. Kitchen with sink, dresser and cupboards and Three bedrooms, one with fireplace and the other with cupboard.*
> *Mains electricity. Estate water.*
> *Outside: Washhouse with copper. Fuel store. E.C.*
> *Well maintained Flower and Kitchen Garden.*

The cottage has been extensively extended and now has four bedrooms and two bathrooms. The former kitchen was made into a sitting room. Apparently, when built, numbers 3 and 4 had adjacent staircases that descended to a shared room, this being either the kitchen or the scullery. There are a number of outbuildings in the large garden.

The cottage used to be that of the estate woodsman.

Number 4 -Woodlands

This is a semi-detached cottage, the southerly of a pair situated on the east side of the road through the village.

The 1956 sale catalogue entry is as follows:

It is stone built with a tiled roof and has metal framed casement windows.
The accommodation comprises:
Entrance porch, Sitting Room with modern tiled fireplace, Living Room, Scullery with sink, dresser and cupboard, Back lobby and Three Bedrooms, one with fireplace.
Mains Electricity. Estate Water.
Outside: Washhouse with copper. Fuel Store. Bucket Closet.
Well - kept Flower and Kitchen Garden.

Like its counterpart number 3, this cottage has also been extensively extended, revealing lath and plaster walls. The staircase that led to the shared room has been moved and the interior rearranged to create larger living spaces. The attic has been converted into accommodation with the half party wall shared with number three being blocked up. The beams appear to be quite old and may have been reused from elsewhere when the property was built.

Number 4 was formerly the home of the estate chaffeur. It is now called Woodlands.

View from the east of, from left, numbers 5, 4 and 3 Hunstrete

Number 5 - Sarah's Cottage

This is a detached stone cottage situated in the centre of Hunstrete on the east side of the road. It is thought to be one of the oldest houses in the village and appears on the 1759 estate map.

The 1956 sale catalogue entry is as follows:

Built of stone with a pantiled roof and contains:
Entrance Hall. Sitting Room with tiled fireplace and dresser. Kitchen with combination range and dresser. Scullery with sink and copper. Pantry with cupboard. Three Bedrooms and Boxroom. Mains electricity and Estate Water.
Outside: Fuel Store and Bucket Closet. Large Flower and Kitchen Garden

The building is understood to have been the village bakery and as such was a meeting place for people, due to its inherent warmth. The house appears to have had two front doors almost adjacent to each other, one of which is blocked up, which are assumed to be one for the cottage and one for the bakery. In the kitchen, the ceiling plaster shows the outline of what is thought to be the old baker's oven. In 1673 there is a bill in the accounts for Hunstrete House, that refers to sweeping the chimney in the baker's house, which may or may not be this building.

Several Victorian pennies have been found in the garden, together with a large quantity of clay pipes and various types of shot and old cartridges. Also discovered was a solid gold livery button, embossed with a hound (see drawing on page 137).

Number 5 has been named Sarah's cottage after Sarah Bailey, a former occupant, who is buried in Compton Dando churchyard.

Number 6 - Bramble Cottage

This is a semi - detached cottage situated in the centre of Hunstrete village on the west side of the road.

The 1956 sale catalogue entry is as follows:

Built of stone with a tiled roof and contains:
Sitting room with fireplace. Pantry. Scullery with copper and cupboard, and Three Bedrooms, one with fireplace.
Mains Electricity. Well and Estate Water.
Good Sized Flower and Kitchen Garden.

Inscribed roof beams in number 6 Hunstreet

This house was bought by the current owners in 1982, who considerably altered and extended it and named it Bramble Cottage. A beam in the attic and almost all the doors have FWLP engraved into them. Some of the roof timbers also have the names or initials of estate workers inscribed on them to celebrate the golden jubilee of Queen Victoria in 1887.

The windows are mostly original with the characteristic Popham panes and catches, although one has thinner bars. This was rescued from the garden of number 7 and used when the house was being extended. The variation may be the result of replicas being used to restore the neighbouring property after a fire. This house and number 7 have been both one and two dwellings at various stages, but are now separate properties again.

The privy halfway down the garden was previously a shared facility as was the 16 feet deep well, which retains water to about half its depth. The orchard has six of the seven original apple trees, one of which is Beauty of Bath. Just to the left of the front gate is an inscribed stone, but the wording has proved impossible to decipher. It looks like J. B. with a date of 1885 or 1888.

Number 6 Hunstrete on the right with number 7 Hunstrete on the left

Number 7 - Orchard Cottage

This is a semi - detached cottage being the farthest of a pair on the west side of the road in the centre of the village.

The 1956 estate sale catalogue describes it as follows:

> *It is built of stone with a tiled roof and contains:*
> *Sitting Room with fireplace. Scullery and Two Bedrooms. Mains electricity. Well and Estate Water.*
> *Outside: Bucket Closet and Fuel Store. Lean - to Washhouse. Front and Back Garden.*

This house is attached to the west end of number 6 but its roof line is lower. It has been greatly extended and is now three bedroomed. On the far end, where the house has been altered, there is a very small Popham window and a date that looks like 1927. There was a fire at this property in the 20th century, which may explain the date above, this being added at rebuilding.

The original front door is now a window, with the new entrance being at the rear of the building. The flagstone floors have been taken up and used to create a large patio. The gardens are extensive but oddly shaped. There is a long thin strip at the front and at the rear they extend across the back of number 8.

Number 8 - Staddlestones

This property is set back on the west side of the road in the centre of Hunstrete.

The 1956 sale catalogue describes it as follows:

> *Built of stone with a tiled roof. It contains:*
> *Sitting room with tiled fireplace and cupboard. Living Room with range.*
> *Scullery with sink, and Three Bedrooms.*
> *Mains Electricity. Estate Water.*
> *Outside: E.C. Coal House. Garden Shed.*
> *Good sized Garden with apple trees.*

Number 8 was formerly the cowman's cottage for Wick Farm. It was renovated about 25 years ago when the sitting room was extended, a back staircase created and three single storey extensions added at the rear. These were a kitchen, a utility room and a storeroom. Local rumour has it that it workmen burnt all the original doors and other fixtures for warmth when the house was being rebuilt. In 1994, several half section Popham windows were found under a pile of builder's rubble and given to 9 Hunstrete to use in building a summerhouse.

In the garden a bottle has been found with the embossed lettering - Genuine Champagne Gingerade, H.J. Walker and Co, Manufacturers by Steam Power, Bath.

It is also known as Staddlestones.

Number 9 - Keeper's Cottage

This was the head gamekeeper's cottage for the Hunstrete Estate. At the time the estate was dispersed in 1956 this was Mr C. E. Fossbury. It is a detached property situated in the centre of the village on the east side of the road. It is bigger than most other houses in Hunstrete and was obviously an important building.

In the 1956 sale catalogue it is described as follows:

> *Built of stone with a tiled roof. The accommodation comprises:*
> *Two Reception Rooms, Four Bedrooms and Bathroom as follows:*
> *Entrance Hall with cupboard. Sitting Room with fireplace and cupboards. Dining Room (S.) with tiled fireplace with back boiler and ample cupboards. Kitchen with sink (hot and cold) and "Glowworm" range with hot water boiler. Bathroom with bath (hot and cold) and low level W.C. suite and Four Bedrooms, one with fireplace.*
> *Outside: Store Shed. Separate W.C.*
> *Mains Electricity, Estate Water. Telephone at present connected.*
> *Excellent Flower and Kitchen Gardens.*
> *The outbuildings include: Lean to Fuel Store. Two Pig - Sties. Game House.*

Four Kennels with runs and Two Kennels with runs.
There is an Orchard to the rear of the garden.

From 1972 the house was used by Holmes Sand and Gravel, a local company owned by 11 brothers, as the hospitality base for a shoot syndicate. It was sold on in 1975. The new purchasers found that the house had no foundations. They also discovered timbers every three feet with red brick between and an outside staircase. This would suggest a much older property than most of those in the village and one that was also different in both building style and materials.

Against the corner of the kitchen was a lean to containing a brick baker's oven with a hatch. There was a milking parlour with an outside niche for a candle and the building may well have been part of the Home Farm at one time. There was also a pump from the well to a water tank in the roof. The walls on the west side are very thick and show an old roof line. There are decoratively carved bargeboards and above the front door an iron lintel with an embossed letter P, presumably standing for Popham. The flagstones that once covered the kitchen floor now form a patio.

The stone outbuilding near the front gate, now being used as a woodcarver's studio, was the former game store. There are numerous hooks in the beams for hanging carcasses from and a flagstone floor and window openings, without glass, to keep the contents cool. The front door is peppered with shot and rumour has it a bird of prey was formerly fixed to the back of it.

When the shoot was still in existence, locals remember the queue of beaters at the front door waiting to be paid. There are the remaining walls of the four dog kennels within which old cupboards from the house were found stored. The other two kennels now lie beneath the garage.

In 1998 the cottage was purchased by the current owners, who have continued to renovate it. The lady of the house tells me that she felt an aura or sensation of grey mist across the corner of the kitchen when she moved in. She sensed it was female, but melancholic and benign. Also she felt it was possibly quite young and may be passing along a path that was established before the house was built. Her husband swore at it and it disappeared, so far never to have returned!

Artefact dug up in the garden of 9 Hunstrete

Two artefacts, the purpose of which is yet to be discovered, were dug up in the garden a few years ago. They are made of brass, highly decorated, and look like knobs of some description.

10 Hunstrete

This is one of a pair of semi detached cottages situated on the road alongside Hunstrete Lake and is the northern one of the two.

Number 10 Hunstrete to the right and number 11 Hunstrete to the left

The 1956 sale catalogue describes it as follows:

> *Built of stone with a gable tiled roof. Contains:*
> *Living room with range, Sitting Room / Kitchen with modern tiled fireplace, deep sink and cupboard, and Two bedrooms, one with hanging cupboard. Outside E.C. and Fuel Store. Garden.*
> *Mains Electricity and Well Water.*

Since then a tiny bathroom has been added to the house and an inside toilet built onto the front. Otherwise the alterations have been relatively few. The house retains its flagstone floors and Popham windows in their solid oak frames. In the roof there are interior walls and in one of the bedrooms are two fireplaces almost next to each other. There is a shed outside with the old toilet, the wash copper and a bread oven.

11 Hunstrete

This is the southern one of a pair of semi detached cottages close to the footpath that runs alongside Hunstrete Lake.

The 1956 estate sale catalogue describes it as follows:

> *Built of stone with a gable tiled roof. Contains:*
> *Sitting room with tiled fireplace and two cupboards, Kitchen with range, dresser and cupboard, Lobby, Scullery with sink and copper and Two bedrooms, each with fireplace and one with alcove. Outside E.C. and Fuel Store.*
> *Mains Electricity and Well Water.*

This house remains virtually unaltered apart from the addition of a stone porch on the side and an extension at the back accommodating a kitchen and bathroom. The decorative quatrefoil in the front gable end is a particular feature.

At one time numbers 10 and 11 were a single property that became two in the 19th century. It may have been completely rebuilt in Victorian times, or an older building renovated, as there is a house on this site on the 1759 Estate map. The style is totally different to any other building in the village and it is Grade II listed (for full entry see appendix 8).

The Estate Saw Mill and Timber Yard

The 1956 Estate Sale Catalogue describes this complex as follows:

> *Situated on the east side of the village public road from which it is approached by a short drive.*
> *There is a Central Yard around which are grouped:*

> *Stone, concrete block, timber and pantiled Saw Mill Building with Rack Saw made by W.B. Haigh Grubun and Co. Ltd. Of Oldham driven by electric motor; second Saw Mill Shed with sliding doors and railway to seasoning yard at rear and Nail and Spares Store.*
> *Two - bay Garage. Three - bay Timber Storage Shed.*
> *Outside: Cement and Gravel Bays.*
> *The Estate Timber Yard is situated in the centre of the buildings.*
> *There is a Seasoning Yard to the west of the Saw Mill building.*

The complex became a stables and riding school after the 1956 sale.

The Gables

Part of the land attached to the former timber yard of the Hunstrete Estate was used as the site of the only completely new built property in the village. This was named The Gables and was used as accommodation for the riding school. It had an equestrian tie that was removed when this closed down.

Sawyer's Mill

Sawyer's Mill prior to renovation

In 1999 the riding school became a livery stable with its owners also buying and selling horses. At this time they converted the main sawmill building into a three bedroomed house called Sawyer's Mill. They have planning permission to extend this, thereby gaining more living space. The outbuildings became two holiday

Sawyer's Mill after renovation with holiday cottages to the left

cottages. They created a garden in the saw mill yard and built a pond in 2003. During this work they found an enormous saw blade and part of the railway track that formerly went to the seasoning yard.

Park Farm

This is described in the 1956 Estate Sale Catalogue as follows:

> *Former dairy farm at the southern end of Hunstrete Village.*
> *Farmhouse*
> *Built of stone with a slate roof. Contains:*
> *Two reception rooms, six bedrooms and bathroom as follows:*
> *Hall with cupboards, Sitting Room 17'×14' 9" with fireplace, Dining Room 17'×15' with tiled fireplace, Living Room 18' 3"×12' 3" with combination stove having hot water boiler, and cupboards. Kitchen with sink (hot and cold). Larder. Back Lobby. Outside Store Room. Lean - to Coal Store. Three Double and Three Single Bedrooms, three with fireplaces. Bathroom with bath (hot and cold), basin (hot and cold) and low level W.C. suite.*
> *Well kept Pleasure and Kitchen Gardens.*
> *Mains Electricity. Estate Water. Septic Tank Drainage.*

Park Farm was sold in the late 1970's with the buildings and land being disposed of separately. The main farmhouse was then split into two properties.

Park Farm and Park Farm Cottage

Park Farm prior to conversion, the front becoming Park Farm and the rear of the building, plus outbuildings, becoming Park Farm Cottage

The front of the farmhouse retained the name Park Farm, whilst the part to the rear became Park Farm Cottage. Each has been the subject of alteration and extension, with the dairy and a cowshed being incorporated into the latter.

The old farmhouse comprised large rooms with high ceilings. The windows had shutters with mouldings on them to match those on the pine doors. Some of wood was embossed with the Popham mark, in this case FWLP. Park Farm contains the former hall complete with flagstone floor. Stairs from the kitchen lead to a large cellar containing a fireplace surmounted by an arch, and also two blocked up doorways.

Park Farm and Park Farm Cottage to the left and Barnwell to the right

Farm Buildings

These are placed to the south of the house and comprise:

> *Grouped around a concrete yard are a brick, stone and pantiled range containing Engine Room with electric pump to drive water to house tank, Cowhouse for nine with concrete standings, chain ties and timber fittings, Dairy, Second Cowhouse for 12 with concrete standings, tubular yoke ties and automatic water bowls and lean - to Boiler House; similar range comprising Cowhouse for three with concrete standings and tubular yoke ties, Fodder Bay, Cowhouse for 11 with stone cobble standings, concrete mangers and feeding passages, tubular yoke ties, automatic water bowls and sliding door, stone and pantiled Stabling of Loose Box, Stalls and Left over; lean - to stone, brick and pantiled range comprising Calving Box and Three Calf Boxes; Stone and pantiled Barn with Fuel Bay, four Calving Boxes and lean - to Shed with door to road. North of the farmhouse is a Rick Yard, stone and pantiled Hay Barn partly converted as Calf Box and two lean - to Chicken Houses.*

The outbuildings were all converted into new properties as follows:

Barnwell

The hay barn to the north, originally in the rick yard attached to the garden of Park Farm, became Barnwell. It was converted prior to the sale of the farm and became a three bedroomed house for the owners, in their retirement. On the south gable end of Barnwell are two dates, 1856 and 1974, which I assume to be the date of the original building and that of the conversion. Its name is an amalgamation of the barn and a well, both of which are situated at the bottom of this wall. Also here is the original pump for the yard (see photograph on page 50).

Stable Cottage, The Barn and Middle Barn

The remaining outbuildings were converted in the late 1970's into the following new properties: Stable Cottage which was the cowshed, Middle Barn which was formerly the stable and part of a cowshed and The Barn from the cartshed.

Outbuildings of Park Farm in 1956

Demolished Properties

Although newer properties are often established on the site of older ones, there are certain houses shown on the 1756 estate map that no longer exist and whose sites have not been built on. Several of these now lie beneath the car parks of the fishing complex, one is beneath the lake, and others are under the gardens of present houses. There is also one, deep in the woods, which was most likely the warrener's house.

The Village Green

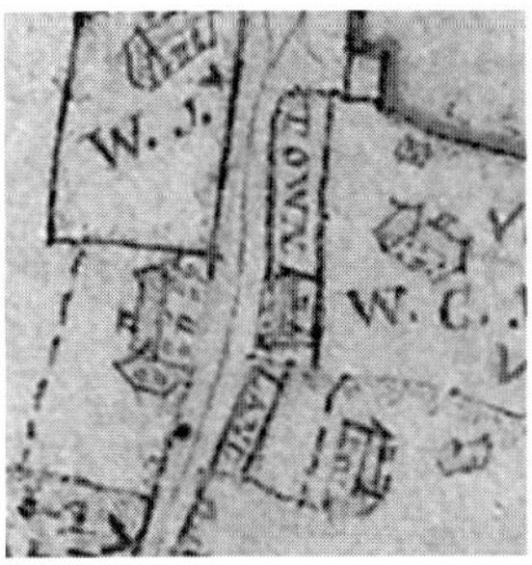

The Green, from the 1759 estate map

There is a tiny village green situated on the east side of the road between houses 5 and 9. This was larger in the past, being shown on the 1759 map as Town Land and acted as a focal point for the village. Parts of it have long since been incorporated into gardens. A payment recorded in the accounts for 1787 refers to hoeing and weeding potatoes on the green. Whether this was the village green or elsewhere remains a mystery!

The horse chestnut tree, on the small patch of village green remaining, was planted in 1941 to mark the birth of Susan Lloyd, the eldest daughter of the former Elizabeth Leyborne Popham and her husband Roger Lloyd. Also here is a bench to commemorate the Portlocks who lived in the village for forty years, from 1940 - 1980. Mr Portlock was the last woodsman for the Hunstrete Estate.

In the 1950's the Mendip Hunt used to meet here as Mrs Buller Leyborne Popham was the master. An older resident particularly remembers that she rode side-saddle. Records show that the village had a pound for the keeping of stray animals. Though no longer in existence, the 1843 Tithe Map shows this as being in the vicinity of the telephone box adjacent to the green. There are several references for the need to repair this in the court rolls. In 1711 there is a mention, in a lease, of a cottage near the pound, however, I am uncertain as to which house this refers, and it may even have been demolished.

It is likely that the stocks and whipping post were also in this central location. I have been unable to locate the site of the village pump, although there is a reference to it in the literature in 1705.

The People of Hunstrete

Information about the inhabitants of Hunstrete, down through the centuries, can be gleaned from a number of sources including court rolls, map schedules, leases, various accounts, employment records and census returns. However these only provide tantalising glimpses, particularly in the more distant past, from which to compile a picture of those that once lived and worked at Hunstrete.

The situation is further complicated by the close proximity of Marksbury, with many records covering both villages, often making accurate identification impossible. Indeed for several centuries they were treated as one manor, becoming separate around 1750. Only occasionally, even in leases and census returns, is Hunstrete specifically referred to by name. From the available sources, so far found, I have compiled a list of the known occupants of the village down through the ages.

Mediaeval Times

Various references occur from time to time in the literature, particularly that pertaining to Glastonbury Abbey. The first person I can find placed specifically in the village is Lady Margeria de Hunderstert, who in 1235 is listed in a survey as a free tenant. The next is Walter Cumyn who is recorded in the Rolls of the Itinerant Justices for the Hundred of Keynsham, dated 1257, as being in dispute with the Abbot of Glastonbury. This concerned common of pasture in Marksbury appertaining to his free tenement in Hundesterte. The same document refers to John de Hundesterte and Richard de Hundesterte.

The Cumyn family, variously spelt Comyn and Cumin in the literature, appear in several leases from 1277 to 1339 when they quitclaimed all rights in Hundestert to the Abbot of Glastonbury. Due to the last mentioned document I believe them to have resided at Hunstrete during this time. The records, as far as I can ascertain, contain no references to specific inhabitants of Hunstrete from now until 1517. From here I have listed the known occupants in each century.

16th century

In 1517 a lease refers to Nicholas Derell who occupied a house called 'Longstabulle'. I have been unable to find where this property was.

In 1536 the baliff for Hundestert and Marksbury, for the Abbey of Glastonbury, is named as Thomas Clowde. His annual fee was 16s 8d.

17th century

In 1637 Jerome Harvey of Houndstreet is recorded as leaving £100 in his will for the poor of Marksbury.

18th century

The records now become more detailed and the inhabitants easier to trace. Documents for this period give an indication of the families that lived in Hunstrete. All of the names below come from leases dated around 1740 but earlier dates were also given as tenancies were normally granted for the period of three lives. The occupants are as follows with the earliest date of tenancy shown to the left of them:

1701 Rebecca Bishop
1706 John Baker
1711 Arthur Collins
1714 William Brookman
1715 John Hardwick
1717 John Brookman
John Hill
1722 John Clement
Joseph Brookman
Joseph Clement
1723 John Shore
John Court
1724 Joseph Quarman
1733 Samuel Boulter
Richard Canvin

The above need to be interpreted carefully, as tenancies were transferable on marriage. For example by 1733 Samuel Boulter was occupying the cottage previously leased to John Hardwick, having wed his daughter.

The 1759 map of the estate (see page 6) has an accompanying schedule that also gives a list of leaseholders. In this case I have been able to match inhabitants with properties, through the relative positions of the houses on the accompanying map. The people and the houses they occupied are as follows:

William Palmer - Number 1
William Bishop - now demolished
George Candy - Hunstrete Cottage
John Brookman - Number 5
Ann Griffis - Number 8
John Collins - now demolished

William Clement - Number 9
John Collins - Number 6/7 (one property)
Joseph Blinman - Park Farm
Roger Hales - now demolished
Samuel Boulter - now demolished
William Brookman - Number 10/11 (one property)
Sarah Wicks - now demolished
John Bishop - now demolished
John Candy - Number 2
John Shoar - now demolished‘

This gives a total of 14 cottages plus Park Farm and Hunstrete Cottage, making 16 households in the village at this time.

In 1702 there is a letter to Richard Cottle, Yeoman, and in 1705 Richard Knott is referred to as a footman at Hunstrete House. In1755 Daniel Green, the Popham's steward, was assigned the house previously occupied by George Canvin. In 1763 there is a lease to George Shoar of Houndstreet, labourer and in 1780 John Brookman's name appears in a document, when his property was sold to Francis Popham.

19th century

In 1807 Walter Prior is the occupant of a

> *cottage and garden adjoining on the north to an orchard late John Hills and on the east to a ground called Houndstreet common*

By 1841 census returns were published, and are available for every subsequent tenth year, until 1901. These make finding out about the occupants of Hunstrete a great deal easier but there are still problems. Once again the village is linked with Marksbury and there seems to be no defined order in which the results were recorded, varying with the different enumerators. Errors were common, particularly in the earlier censuses, with names and ages often being incorrectly recorded, so caution is needed when interpreting the results.

The census returns show that Hunstrete House was occupied in 1841 by Edward Langford, the rector of Marksbury and by Charles Andrew in 1851 and 1861.The situation then becomes unclear from 1871 to 1891 with it being recorded as uninhabited in 1881. In the returns for 1901 the tenant is listed as Wodehouse. The lists also inform us that Hunstrete Cottage was lived in by the following estate agents:

1841 - Thomas Pointing until

1881- Andrew Patterson

1891 - Charles Baker

1901 - Robert Pierce

Very rarely, unless important, can a house be specifically identified. The only property, apart from the two above, that I can be certain of is number 9 as it was the home of the Braine family, gamekeepers, for over 70 years. However, by using other means such as the 1843 tithe map, which was compiled to show dues owed to the church, a record of some inhabitants can be established. The tithe award enables the following households to be pinpointed:

Thomas Pointing - Hunstrete Cottage

Albert Neal - Number 1

John King - Number 5

John Bees - Numbers 6 and 7 and possibly 8

Samuel Brain - Number 9

James Taylor - Numbers 10 and 11

Charles Keedwell - Park Farm

Number 2 Hunstrete seems to be part of the timber yard formerly located here.

20th century

The only census return available for this century is that of 1901. It is easier to follow than previous ones, seeming to take a logical route round the village. It lists the following heads of household:

Thomas Hayter - Number 1

James Deacon - Number 2

Robert Pierce - Hunstrete Cottage

Sophie Hawker - Number 3

Sidney Hillier - Number 4

Harry Bates - Number 5

Samuel Barnes - Numbers 6 and 7

James Nash - Number 8

Henry Breen- Number 9

Thomas Rosewell - Number 10

Uninhabited - Number 11

Hunstrete House - Wodehouse, a tenant

I have been fortunate in being given a complete list of occupants of Hunstrete circa 1939 compiled by Tony Gill whose relations lived in the village. They were as follows:

From left: Ann, Mary and Elizabeth Leyborne Popham

Hunstrete House: Mr F. W. L. Popham, known as 'Pop' to his employees, Mrs Popham and their three daughters Elizabeth, Mary and Anne. The indoor staff included the cook, the governess, the housemaid, the nursemaid, the parlourmaid, the kitchen maid and the sewing maid. Ernest Barnes, the head gardener, lived in part of the wing that is now the suites.

Hunstrete Cottage: Mr Gasgoine who had staff comprising a gardener and his wife, employed as a housekeeper.

Number 1: Edgar Smith, farm worker, Ciss his wife and their daughters Margaret, Rosalie and Sheila.

Number 2: Charlie Deacon, estate worker and tractor driver, his wife Maude, their sons Bill and Ken and daughter Dorothy.

From left: Nellie Parsons, Albert Parsons, Jack Parsons, Ernest Barnes (stepson), Alice Parsons, Joan Parsons

Number 3: Jack Parsons, coal miner, his wife Alice and their son Jack who worked on the estate. Their daughters Joan and Nell had married and left home by this time.

Number 4: Vick Hunt, the Popham's chauffeur, his wife Winnie and their daughters Pauline, Jean and Diana.

Number 5: Jim Deacon, head estate worker, his wife Alice and her sister Sarah Bailey.

Number 6: Sam Barnes, coal miner and later road worker, His wife Elizabeth and their seven children. Their sons were Ernest, boot boy, later quarry worker and then road worker, Sidney who was a carpenter, Leslie who was the Popham's kennel man and Reg who was the poultry man. Henry the eldest had been killed in action in World War I aged 19. Their daughters were Win, who was the Popham's sewing maid, Gwen and Isobel, usually known as Bet.

From left: Lydia Bees and daughters outside number 7 Hunstrete

Number 7: Harry Bees, estate worker, his wife Lydia and their daughters Elsie and Louise. Both girls were severely retarded and because of this Mrs Bees never went outside the village in more than thirty years.

Number 8: Enoch Prior, estate gardener, his wife Mary and their sons Tom, who was a farm worker and Jack. Their daughters Florence, Frances and Margery had married and left home by this time.

Number 9: Charlie Trussler, estate gamekeeper, his wife, their son Keith and daughters Peggy and Joyce. Previous to this in the mid 1930's the occupants had been George Rawlings, his wife, and their children Frank, Fred, Arthur, Nell, Kate, Eva and Rose.

Number 10: Bill Rosewell, coal miner, his wife and their children Mabel, George, Margery, Joan and Betty.

Number 11: Dick Palmer, estate worker, his wife Nellie and their daughter Nellie.

Park Farm: Wilfred Himmens, the farm manager, his wife Jane and their children John and June. They had started married life at 1 Hunstrete. Mr Himmens' father was farm manager before him.

From left: Edgar Smith, Douglas Young, Mary Wilson, Wilfred Himmens

After the estate was sold in 1956 the existing houses became privately owned and many have changed hands several times. Also various new properties were developed, so I have not listed any inhabitants after this date.

The villagers would have attended Marksbury church and many of the names associated with the village can be found both in the parish records and engraved on headstones in the churchyard. For example, John Farmer, a land steward, is recorded for posterity as follows

> *Sacred to the Memory of*
> *John Farmer Jun.*
> *who died April 23rd 1822*
> *Aged 36 years*
>
> *He served several years as Land Steward*
> *to General Popham at Houndstreet*
> *Died respected by his Neighbours*
> *and will be long lamented by his Relatives.*

Throughout the ages Hunstrete was farmed, initially using the mediaeval open field system, evidence of which can be seen at nearby Wick Farm. This was a separate manor, with its own house and chapel, until becoming part of the Popham estates in the early 17th century. Here the sharp bend, adjacent to the entrance, is attributed to the road following the original lines of the open field system.

The land was owned by the lord of the manor and worked by the villeins. In the mediaeval system of tenure these were the unfree tenants, bound to the land and required to provide labour. For example in 1258, in the adjacent manor to Hunstrete, Alicia de Wyke held one house with its curtilage, together with one acre and rights in the common fields. She paid a rent of 12d per year and was required to work at weeding and haymaking, this being worth 1½d. Richard Fogzel held the same, and Robert Muling held one tenement for which he paid 6d per annum in rent. The services of the villeins were transferable, should the manor be leased.

The tenants at Hunstrete are recorded as having to collectively pay 6s each year at the feast of the Nativity of the Blessed Virgin (8th September), towards the running costs of the monks' kitchen at Glastonbury.

The land attached to the manor, suitable for farming, would have been divided into two or three large, unfenced, common fields. The villeins would have had strips scattered randomly in each to ensure a fair distribution of the varying types of soil and accompanying productivity. These were cultivated on a three year rotational system to maintain fertility. One field was planted with wheat or rye sown in the autumn, another with barley or oats sown in the spring, whilst the third was left fallow, being rested for a year after the stubble had been grazed.

Turning animals into the field after the crop had been harvested also ensured that it was manured. Under good management, land left fallow would be ploughed three times during the summer to kill weeds and to improve the soil structure. A small area of peas, beans or vetches might be sown in the cereal fields to provide variety in the diet.

Any land not used for arable crops or as meadow, was either woodland or used as common pasture upon which each holding was entitled to graze a specified number of livestock. Houndstreet Common is referred to in 1539 as being one mile and is shown on a map of 1806 (see page 7) as situated, at least in part, to the east of the village.

Meadowlands or meads were fertile, low lying, well-watered lands often adjoining a watercourse. They were usually fairly level for ease of mowing with a scythe. After haymaking was completed, usually by Lammas Day (1st August) , meadowland was treated as pasture and grazed in common by the village livestock. The villagers also had certain rights in the woodland. The monastic survey of 1517 stated that the villeins of Marksbury and Hunstrete were able to graze their cattle in Lez Holte or the Common Wood between The Feast Of The Purification (2nd February) and Hocktide (2nd Tuesday after Easter).

Transgressions of accepted practices were taken seriously and brought before the court. The following examples from the court rolls show the most common of these

> *1727 We present any commoner that lets any common and puts in stock himself to forfeit five pounds*
>
> *John Bishop for continued encroachment against the Hoult gate*
>
> *1731 No tenant can stock on the common more than one horse and as many cattle as they can maintain on the tenement*

In 1809 William Taylor was paid 12s 6d for

> *Serving Notices and distribute handbills relating to setting on fire and cutting up the furze on the different commons.*

Whether this was to prevent this, or instruct the villagers to do so, is difficult to ascertain as it could be either. Furze is also known as gorse and unless controlled can be very invasive. It was often used to fire bread ovens due to the heat it generates when burnt.

With changing practices of land management the open fields were enclosed and replaced by individual farms. How many there were is unclear although those most referred to in documentary evidence are Wick Farm and Park Farm at Hunstrete. The former features several times in the accounts as follows

> *1790 Bill for thatching at Wick Farm*
>
> *1791 Bill for 2 loads of tiles at Wick Farm*
>
> *1793 Building a new oven at Wick Farm*
>
> *1794 John Holbrook for thatching at Wick Farm*

This suggests that at the time it was undergoing a period of renovation or rebuilding. It is likely that all but the demesne farm, variously referred to as Home Farm, Hunstrete Farm and Park Farm in the documentation, were tenanted.

Various snippets of information, with regard to farming practices, can be gleaned from the documentary evidence. A lease of 1702 refers to

> *All that outlet used for the feeding of pigs and poultry...and the barnes and ox house near adjoining.*

This tells us the animals that were kept, as does payment for the following items in 1773, being indicative of a dairy herd: *A lead for a cheese press, a new cheese tub, a stand for the cheese tub, cheese tongs and a barrel churn.* These also confirm the production of both cheese and butter. The accounts also record several purchases of sheep.

The various tasks carried out on the farms can also be discovered from the account books. In 1713 a payment was made for ploughing, but is the only record of this I can find anywhere. The ploughs were wooden and pulled by oxen or horses. In 1807 helm for thatching is mentioned in the accounts and in 1810 the sum of £10 10s 0d was spent on helm used at Wick Farm. This is also spelt yealm and is the term for a bundle of thatching material. It was the most common form of roof covering for centuries and in this area was carried out using straw, that would have been harvested locally as a by product of wheat production.

Harrowing at Hunstrete c. 1928

Thatched Hayrick c. 1910

In 1811 John Cantle was paid £1 7s 0d for thatching three hayricks. This was the tried and tested method of protecting the crop and continued well into the 1940's at Hunstrete.

The records also tell us what crops were grown at Hunstrete. In 1807 a report recommends that 80 acres below the keeper's house be used as a farm. It suggests that wheat, oats, clover and turnips be grown and that the only additional buildings needed would be a small barn and stables (see appendix 12). This seems to have occurred as two such buildings were constructed in the park in 1824 and the field books show the following regime for Redfield:

Carting hay and building a haystack c. 1910

1829 Wheat
1830 Barley
1831 Fallow, then potatoes
1832 Barley
1833 Clover, mown, turnips and potatoes
1834 Clover and wheat

In 1810 Michael Cutler was paid £2 10s 0d for quarrying stones and digging foundations for a lime kiln at Chelworth Park Farm. Lime was spread on the fields to control the acidity of the soil. It was obtained by crushing limestone and burning it to produce a white powder. It was also used into make mortar for building work and as an ingredient of plaster, so kilns were commonplace.

In 1884 there is a payment to a man and three women for cutting Meadow Saffron on Hunstrete Farm. This is commonly known as Autumn Crocus. It is a perennial plant with the root being a bulb and is unusual in that the leaves appear and wither before the plant flowers in September. The bulb contains a strong poison but it was recommended, in old herbals, to be worn round the neck in a bag to prevent or cure fevers. Whether it was a crop or the harvesting refers to wild specimens is unclear. It may have been grown as a dye plant or for the use of its stamens in colouring food. It is now a relatively rare wild plant, but is common in the Hunstrete area.

Fern or bracken was a problem in pastureland and had to be controlled. In 1813 John Filer was paid the sum of £1 0s 0d for mowing fern. In 1814 a note appears in the accounts recording the payment of a deodand, or compensation, to the value of 13s 0d, on the death of Joseph Pinn, who was killed by a load of fern falling on him.

Similarly stones rising to the surface caused problems in arable fields and were controlled by stone picking. This backbreaking task was usually carrried out by women and children. The accounts show two payments for this work. In 1815 Samuel Braines two girls were paid 4s 9d for four days picking stones and in 1817 the same children received 16s for 16 days work, a rate of 1s a day. The stones were usually piled at the side of the road to be collected later and used in lime kilns or for road repairs.

The control of vermin was another regular task for which numerous payments appear in the accounts. This was principally for the killing of both moles and rabbits. In 1713 Edward Hart received the sum of 8s 0d for killing eight dozen moles making the going rate 1s 0d per dozen. By 1806 when the molecatcher was paid £1 10s 0d for 15 dozen moles, the rate had increased to 2s 0d per dozen.

The payment for rabbits in 1806 was 2s 6d per couple making them 15s 0d per dozen. The much higher rate for rabbits was probably due to the fact that these could be sold at market, thereby recouping some of the cost of controlling their numbers. The accounts record £143 0s 0d worth being sold to a Mr Davies of Bristol in 1820. No further sales seem to have taken place after 1821, probably due to the report of 1807 that recommended the removal of the warren (for full report see appendix 12).

The usual method of capture appears to be netting, as the 1806 accounts record payment for twine for knitting a rabbit net. This involved placing nets over all but one of the holes in a rabbit warren and sending a dog down the remaining one. The fleeing animals made for the nearest exit and ran straight into the nets, from which they were removed and subsequently killed. There is also a reference to ferrets in the documentation, which were also used for this purpose.

Alcohol, to keep the workers refreshed, was an important consideration on the farms. In 1806 James Noble was paid the sum of £6 16s 0d for supplying malt and hops to brew beer for haymaking. By 1809 the supplier was Abraham James and the cost had risen to £8 8s 8d! Cider was also made regularly on the Hunstrete estate, from early on. Records for the eighteenth century show a payment for 20 sacks of apples for cider. Tony Gill gives the following account of this happening in the late 1930's

> *Cider was made in large quantities in the sawyard. Wooden farm waggons were parked in the various orchards and piled high with apples knocked from the trees with poles and gathered by hand. Leaves, twigs, bird droppings and the occasional mouse all went in the cider press. They don't make it like that today!*
>
> *All estates and farms made cider then to attract the extra labour needed at times of haymaking and harvesting.*

Gillian Barnes, who lived with her parents in the gardener's cottage at Hunstrete House in the 1940's, recalls large barrels of cider being kept at the rear of the waggon shed, now the maintenance store. One barrel was always on tap from which the estate workers were allowed to help themselves.

In the 1930's Hunstrete had a herd of imported Jersey cattle, being one of the first farms in the country to keep this breed. They were prize winning pedigree animals and included Hunstrete Volunteer Emperor, Hunstrete Sarkie's Volunteer and Hunstrete Empress Doreen. The cattle were kept primarily for their milk and the production of cream and butter. When Hugh Leyborne Popham died in 1943 the Jersey herd was sold and the farm manager Mr Himmens and his family moved to Chewton Keynsham.

At the time of the dispersal of the estate in 1956 there were four farms: Park Farm in Hunstrete which was the Home Farm, Wick Farm just to the north of the village, and Church Farm and Whidcomb Farm in Marksbury. These were all run as dairy farms and were 129 acres, 266 acres, 249 acres and 207 acres respectively. Their sale brought to an end many centuries of farming on the Hunstrete estate.

Jersey Bull outside Hunstrete House in 1920

Timber Production

Timber production has always been one of the main functions of the Hunstrete Estate. Collinson in his 1791 'History and Antiquities of the County of Somerset' quotes a Glastonbury Abbey survey of 1293 which says

> *Also there are apperteynyng unto the saide mannor, certayne woods, called Haywood, Newood, and the Common, set with okes and ashes of dyvers kyndes, the acres whereof cannot be esteemed, for they growe in plots, valued at this survey to be worth £106 19s 8d, whereof may be made a yerely wood sale of 60s.*

This confirms timber production on the estate from at least the 13th century, although it was probably carried out from the 10th century, when it was acquired by Glastonbury Abbey. In 1785 there is a payment for making faggots and logs and in 1786 for cording 16 cord of wood.

The felling of trees was carried out by hand with the timber being moved by horses. The Labour and Wages Book for 1883 - 84 records numerous payments to William Ruddle for the use of horses to haul timber.

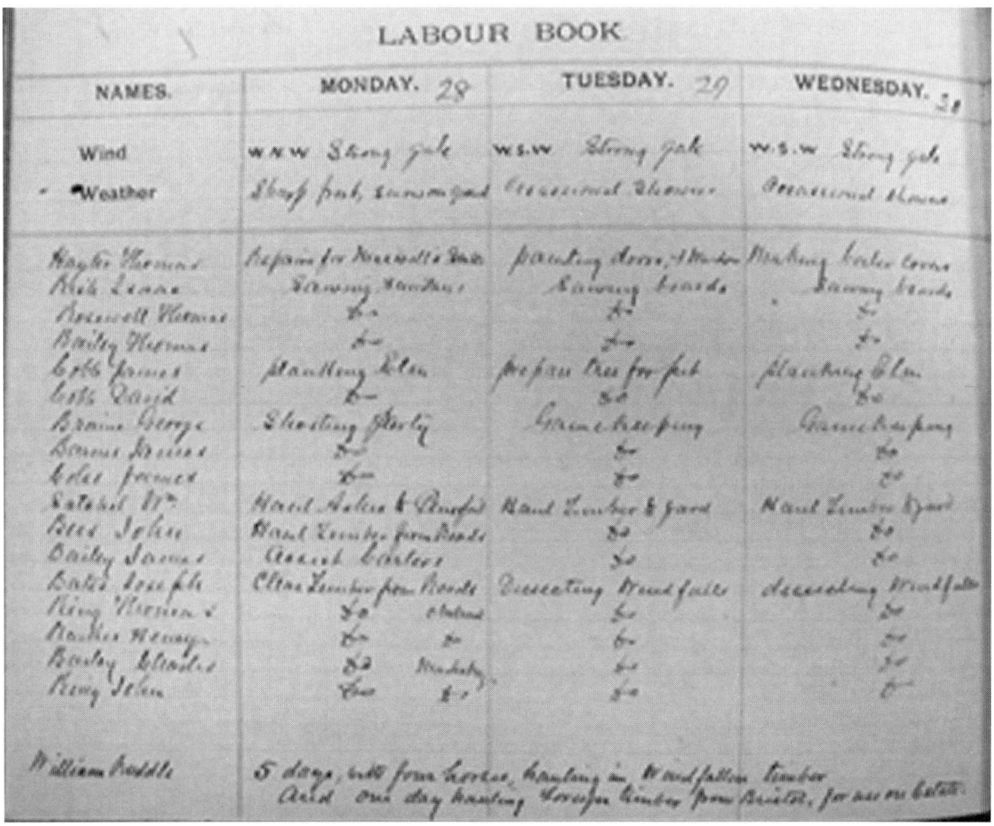

The Labour and Wages Book for 1883-84 showing hauling of timber by horses, at the bottom of the page

The Hunstrete Estate had its own wood yard and sawmills and tasks listed for this in the same document include:

Hauling elm
Preparing trees for the pit
Pit sawing oak
Planking oak and elm
Sawing elm board
Sawing fencing and fence posts
Sawing joisting and rafters
Putting and barking oak

Sawing by means of a pit was a dirty and tiring job. It involved two men manipulating a long handled saw. One man operated the end above ground whilst the one holding the lower end was below ground and inevitably got covered in sawdust. In 1807 George Cobb was paid £49 2s 5d for sawyer's work in that year and Samuel Baber £1 7s 6d for lifting 11 cord of wood from the sawpit.

Eventually hand sawing was replaced by machine and older residents of the area can still recall the steam driven engine. Tony Gill provided the following account of the sawmill in the late 1930's

> *A steam engine, the type of traction engine now seen at steam festivals, was anchored to a concrete base and attached by a long belt to a large circular saw (about four or five feet in diameter), which could cut anything from fence posts to medium sized trees.*
>
> *Work was allowed to accumulate to make it worthwhile 'firing up' the engine for a few days work for a team of men. Safety precautions amounted to somebody shouting "Watch that bloody belt."*
>
> *When trees were cleared in large numbers, or giant trees were involved, contractors with special tractors and winches were employed. One such team, three Welshmen, lived for weeks by Hunstrete lake in a caravan (a wooden hut on cast iron wheels).*
>
> *Local boys found it fascinating to watch powerful state of the art tractors at work, after the small and relatively gentle Fordson agricultural machine belonging to the estate.*
>
> *Two shire horses (named Nan and Darling I believe) handled the smaller timber.*

Much of the timber produced was used on the estate, making it virtually self sufficient in this resource. Carpenters and joiners are recorded in the previously mentioned book as:

Making mantel shelf for 201
Making well covers
Making closet seat
Making doors and door frames
Making window frames
Making 15000 spekes for thatching

Horses being used to haul timber at Hunstrete House after the gale of 1928

These items were for use in the cottages and farmhouses of the estate, as the above records show. Indeed many still survive a testament to the quality of workmanship of the day. Some can be positively identified by the initials EWLP or FWLP burned into the finished item. This dates items in the former case to 1804 - 1843 and in the latter to 1880 - 1907. The marks were used particularly on door braces, and lintels and stair treads and risers.

According to the schedule for the 1843 tithe map the timber yards were located where the estate builders' yard was in the 20th century. They were moved, to just below the lake, sometime in the latter half of the 19th century.

In 1956 when Hunstrete was disposed of by the Popham family, the sawmills ceased production and the buildings were converted to holiday cottages and a private house; their former function living on in the name Sawyer's Mill. The yard is now the garden, stables and an indoor training arena for horses.

Hunstrete Estate sawmill c. 1936

Gamekeeping

The keeping of game for hunting was practised at Hunstrete from at least AD936 when the Anglo Saxon charter refers to the boundary game enclosure. The earliest inhabitants would therefore have been involved in gamekeeping. In a survey of 1239 a charter of free warren, granted by King Edward, was recorded. This confirmed the right to hunt within the manor and therefore the employment of people to manage the game.

The duties of the gamekeeper would have included maintaining the deer herd and also the rabbit warren. They would also have had responsibility for protecting the game from being stolen. Poaching particularly of deer, hares, rabbits and fish, was a regular occurrence on the estate. Bonds, whereby offenders were bound over not to reoffend on penalty of an agreed sum, were used as a deterrent in the 18th century. A list of Game Preservation and General Estate Management Bonds exists for 1730 – 1802. It forbids the use of the following devices:

> *setting dog, Spanish lurcher, greyhound, gun, net, harepipe, engine snare or harness for killing, catching, destroying or disturbing game.*

Some of the many entries are as follows:

> *1730 John Long of Compton Dando - bond not to destroy Mr Francis Popham's game*
>
> *1736 James Perry of Midsomer Norton - bond not to disturb Mr Edward Popham's game*
>
> *1740 Thomas Teague of Publow - bond not to fish in any of the rivers, rivulets or brooks belonging to Mr Edward Popham or kill or destroy any hares, rabbits or other game whatsoever in his manors*
>
> *1754 William Brookman of Houndstreet – bond not to destroy Mr Edward Popham's game. Sum of ten pounds of good and lawful money of Great Britain. Killed a male deer.*
>
> *Note: William Brookman lately molested, abused and threatened the life of Thomas Allwood Warrener and gamekeeper of the said Mr Popham and disturbed the game. Allwood was pleased to forbear prosecution as the offence was acknowledged and William Brookman bound not to offend in the like manner for the future.*

In the 19th and 20th centuries pheasants and partridges became far more important than either deer or rabbits. Duties for the gamekeeper in the 1883 - 84 Labour and Wages book included getting up barley for pheasants, hauling barley to covers, partridge shooting and ferreting rabbits.

The importance of gamekeeping on the estate, particularly in the above mentioned centuries is indicated by the allocation of two cottages to house gamekeepers. The head keeper's house was number 9 Hunstrete and the second keeper's Wood View in Compton Dando. Both properties are considerably larger than most others in the village.

The first keeper identifiable by name was the previously mentioned Thomas Allwood in 1754. The 1841 census tells us that by this time the keeper was Samuel Braine aged 60. His son George, aged 25, was listed as following the same occupation. By 1851 he had succeeded his father, who had become a gardener. George remained keeper for over well over 30 years. By 1891, his own son Henry, had assumed the role, continuing a long family tradition and was still there in 1901.

By the late 1930's the head keeper was Charlie Trussler. He served the Popham family for 21 years. His son, Keith, told me that his father's duties included the rearing of pheasants and partridges for the shooting season and the control of vermin. The dead animals or birds would be hung on fences in specific locations, so that when his employer walked round he could see that the job was being carried out properly. All this had to be done on foot, including the carrying of feedstuffs, on an estate of approximately 3 000 acres.

Charlie Trussler the Gamekeeper c.1936

The rearing of pheasants was a major part of the job. In the spring the birds would be enticed into pens with food. They found their way in easily but couldn't get out! The gamekeeper would then collect up the female birds and put them in cages with the cocks. As the eggs were laid they were removed and put under broody hens kept in coops. When the eggs hatched the hens were tethered to allow them to eat but not desert the chicks. The pens were laid out in rows in the field below Keeper's Cottage and moved regularly to prevent disease building up. They were spaced 20 yards apart to prevent the hens attacking stray chicks from another brood.

The keeper would let the hen and chicks out at first light and stay with them all day to prevent losses to predators. At dusk he then had to shut them in. When the pheasant chicks were six to eight weeks old they were moved to the woods. The night before this happened the keeper would put a sack under the coop and the next morning lift the whole thing and transport it intact.

Gamekeeper and assistant with horse drawn caravan

The pens would be put in a ride and the chicks and hens released. The latter would be collected some weeks later, when the young birds were mature enough to roost in the trees, and returned to the farm from which they been borrowed. The chicks would be fed in the woods by the keeper, who often stayed in a caravan. This was horse drawn and very basic. The shooting season began on the 1st October and ended on the 1st February. The whole process would then begin again.

The gamekeeper also organised shoot days on approximately 10 - 12 occasions each year. This involved employing the right number of beaters and organising them, supervising the guests during the shoot and dealing with the dead game at the end of the day.

Beaters at a Hunstrete shoot c.1936

Tony Gill sent me the following account of shoots in the late 1930's, for which Trussler would have been responsible. It brings the occasion vividly to life:

> *On Saturdays in winter, wealthy men, looking like latter day Edward VII's in tweeds and plus fours, with tiny brightly coloured feathers, mostly from jays, in their hat bands, would arrive in large cars with ornate and very expensive hand made guns, usually twelve bores.*
>
> *Hours before, in darkness, beaters would gather to be briefed by keepers on the days shoot, like NCO's being briefed for battle by officers. There was no shortage of volunteers because pay was good. As an eight year old I received one shilling, about two weeks normal pocket money. (Men, I believe, could earn more than ten shillings.)*
>
> *Boys and novices were usually allocated places at intervals (100 yards or so) alongside woods to drive back any wandering game birds. They were allowed to light small fires to keep warm.*
>
> *When the guns were in place at the end of the wood, gangs of experienced beaters crunched noisily through, often making whooping noises, to herd the birds towards the guns.*

Pheasants, reared in their thousands by keepers, then released into the wild, were the main targets. Other creatures, partridges etc, could be taken, but only on the wing.

Etiquette decreed that shooting a songbird, or any bird on the ground, was disgraceful and deserving of the sporting equivalent of a court martial.

On the other hand, shooting a snipe or a woodcock in their fast, erratic, flight demonstrated great skill, the equivalent of a hole in one on the golf course.

Shooters usually had two or more guns and an assistant to carry and load them.

Poaching by local people continued, being commonplace in the first half of the 20th century. One person recalls, in his youth, creeping into the woods at night to bag a pheasant or two for the pot. The method used was to locate oneself beneath a roosting bird, release poisonous fumes by pouring water on carbide, and wait for it to fall unconscious, out of the trees!

Hugh and Janet Leyborne Popham at Hunstrete shoot c.1920

When the estate was sold in 1956 Trussler stayed on for a while as gamekeeper to various syndicates. These included Butler's Tar and the Brown brothers who owned a Bristol company called Holmes Sand and Gravel. Both pheasants and duck were shot but the latter was stopped in the 1960's, being regarded as inhumane by Lady Chancellor. The reason for this was that any wild duck on the lake flew off low and fast thus avoiding the guns, whilst the tamer birds, bred by the estate, flew round and round in confusion, thereby providing easy targets. Trussler eventually moved to Dyrham Park, near Bath and was succeeded by various keepers including George Hinton.

The current letting of the shooting rights in Hunstrete Plantation continues the long sporting tradition of the estate. However with its anticipated sale this will come to an end.

Mining

The area, west of Bath, in which Hunstrete is situated, lies within the North Somerset coalfield. The coal was formed in the Carboniferous period and locally tended to be between one and a half and two feet thick. These thin seams, often undulating in nature, made mining both difficult and dangerous. Initially coal was dug from the few outcrops at the surface during the early 15th century. Only small amounts of coal were produced, mainly for local use, as the majority of people relied on wood for fuel.

As the population increased, this became scarce and the changeover to coal gained impetus. There was a significant rise in output during the mid 17th century when the first vertical shafts were sunk. Mining locally continued to expand reaching its height in 1900 - 1920. The difficult working conditions of the Somerset coalfield were such that local miners were reputed to be the best in the world.

The Popham family used coal to heat their home relatively early on. The 1646 inventory of Francis Popham's possessions at the time of his death itemises *two cole horses*, presumably for haulage purposes and an account of 1713 records payment for 32 sacks of coal for the house at Houndstreet at a cost of £1 12s 0d.

The Pophams were involved in mining both as landowners and as a speculative venture. In 1678 Alexander Popham granted a coal mining lease for the manors of Marksbury and Hunstrete, to Lambrook Long the elder, Lambrook Long the younger and Christopher Dollings, all of Compton Dando. This lease was renewed in 1703. Where they mined is unclear but it was either in Common Wood or Lord's Wood, both of which contain old workings

In 1765 Edward Popham, lord of the manor of Timsbury, granted a 21 year lease to Jacob Mogg, Alexander Adams and John Bush. They sunk a shaft in the area naming it Old Grove. This colliery ceased production in 1878.

A document of 1705 records payment for free shares of coal in Sutton, the Park and Birchwood collieries. Other records show that Heighgrove colliery, near High Littleton, was founded in 1753 by the aforementioned John Bush, and taken over in 1771 by the Heighgrove Coal Company of which the Popham family were shareholders.

The colliery comprised three sites: Heighgrove, Heighgrove Engine and Woody Heighgrove. Together they produced between 9 000 and 135 000 tons of coal per year in the mid 18th century. The royalties from here, known in Somerset as the free share, comprised one eighth the value of the total output, with coal retailing at 3d a bushel, eventually rising to 4d by 1756, and were paid half yearly. From April to October 1771 this amounted to £325 12s 9d. The Popham papers record the last of these freeshare payments to the estate in 1819.

Production also continued on the Hunstrete Estate. An account book of 1705 records free shares of coal in Houndstreet park of £6 9s 5d together with a reference to coal in Birchwood and Timsbury. In 1823, 1824 and 1826 payments are recorded towards the new coal works at Houndstreet.

On 18th March 1829 Messrs. Langford, Hill and James took out leases for coal in the Hunstrete area. In a letter to Edward Popham dated May 1832 it states

> *We despair of finding coal at Houndstreet because of the difficult strata, we wish to abandon the entire venture.*

The above quote echoes the problems found throughout the Somerset coalfield. They were responsible for its ultimate demise with the last collieries to close being Writhlington and Radstock in 1973, bringing to an end 500 years of mining in the area. Two Hunstrete villagers are listed in the census returns as miners, John Shore in 1841 and Sam Barnes in 1901. Tony Gill told me that there were three in the late 1930's: Jack Parsons, the aforementioned Sam Barnes and Bill Rosewell.

Miners about 1925
Left, Bill Ford and right Stanley Bates of Compton Dando, centre Bill Rosewell of Hunstrete

In 1967 rumours began to circulate in Hunstrete of a new mine planned for Common Wood. Exploratory work commenced in 1969 being undertaken by Gasex, Mining Engineers Limited, a family firm from the Radstock area. Testing was carried out prior to obtaining a licence from the National Coal Board to open a private colliery. Planning permission was granted for an initial period of seven years with certain conditions imposed. These were no spoil tips to be made on site and a maximum of 30 people to be employed in situ.

One trial proved unsuccessful whilst another in August 1969 found coal, thought to be equivalent to the Sylving seam at Radstock series, but also uncovered unsuspected workings of the mid 18th century, making mining uneconomic. In October 1969 all working stopped for the winter and a decision was made to cease exploration at the site.

In February 1979 a renewal of planning permission was sought by Gasex. This involved drift mining in a steep sided stream valley known as Hunstrete Bottom. A father and son team applied to mine 5 000 tons of coal annually for distribution in local markets. The villagers of Hunstrete opposed this on the grounds of noise intrusion, extra traffic and the effect on the flora and fauna of Common Wood. Wansdyke planners also opposed it, stating it would be an eyesore in an area of outstanding natural beauty and be inappropriate use of green belt land. They also supported the concerns re noise and traffic. The application was turned down, by the then Avon County Council, on environmental grounds in March 1979.

Whilst ploughing in the 1980's in the field between the Hawhaw and Lord's Wood, Brian Maggs uncovered a large hole. The National Coal Board was called in and declared that it was former mine workings. It took five to six lorry loads of rubble to fill it in.

Law and Order

From the earliest times Hunstrete, in common with every other place in the country, was subject to the laws of the land. In 1256 the courts of the Hundred of Keynsham, an administrative unit of government, were involved in two incidents concerning Hunstrete. The first was

> *Henry de Stanton is accused of robbery in Ferberg (Farmborough) and in Hundesterte, whereof a certain Margery, who was bound, appealed him, comes and defends the whole and puts himself on the country for good and ill. And twelve jurors and four townships of Stanton (Prior), Preston (Priston), Chaleworth (Chelwood) and Cumton (Compton Dando) say positively that he is not guilty. Therefore let him be liberated and under pledge.*

The second is

> *Walter Cumyn, who brought a assize of novel disseisin against the Abbot of Glaston concerning common of pasture in Markbyr(Marksbury) which appertains to his free tenement in Hundesterte, comes and withdraws himself. Therefore he and his pledges to prosecute, namely, John de Hundesterte and Richard de Hundesterte are in mercy. Pledges for Walter's amercements: Nicholas Boyvin of Kattkote and Roger son of Richard de Mere.*

This was in effect a dispute over land, where the tenant felt that he had been unjustly ejected from his property.

Beside these, there were local laws enforced by manorial courts. These were originally oral in nature and proceedings only began to be recorded around the mid 13th century.

Every lord of the manor had the right to hold a court for his tenants and there were two types. One, the Court Baron, dealt with the transfer of copyhold land on inheritance or sale, determined the custom of the manor and enforced payment of services due to the lord. It was normally held every three weeks. The other, the Court Leet, dealt with petty law and order and the administration of communal agriculture. This was normally held every six months. However in practice these functions were not always distinct. Rack, writing around 1770, stated that a Court Baron was held at the Great House twice a year and that the Court Leet had been discontinued.

The courts were presided over by the lord's steward, or reeve, with the proceedings being recorded on long strips of parchment, known as court rolls. The earliest surviving one of these for Hunstrete is dated 1657 and the latest 1795 although the series is incomplete. However these are almost impossible to decipher until 1726.

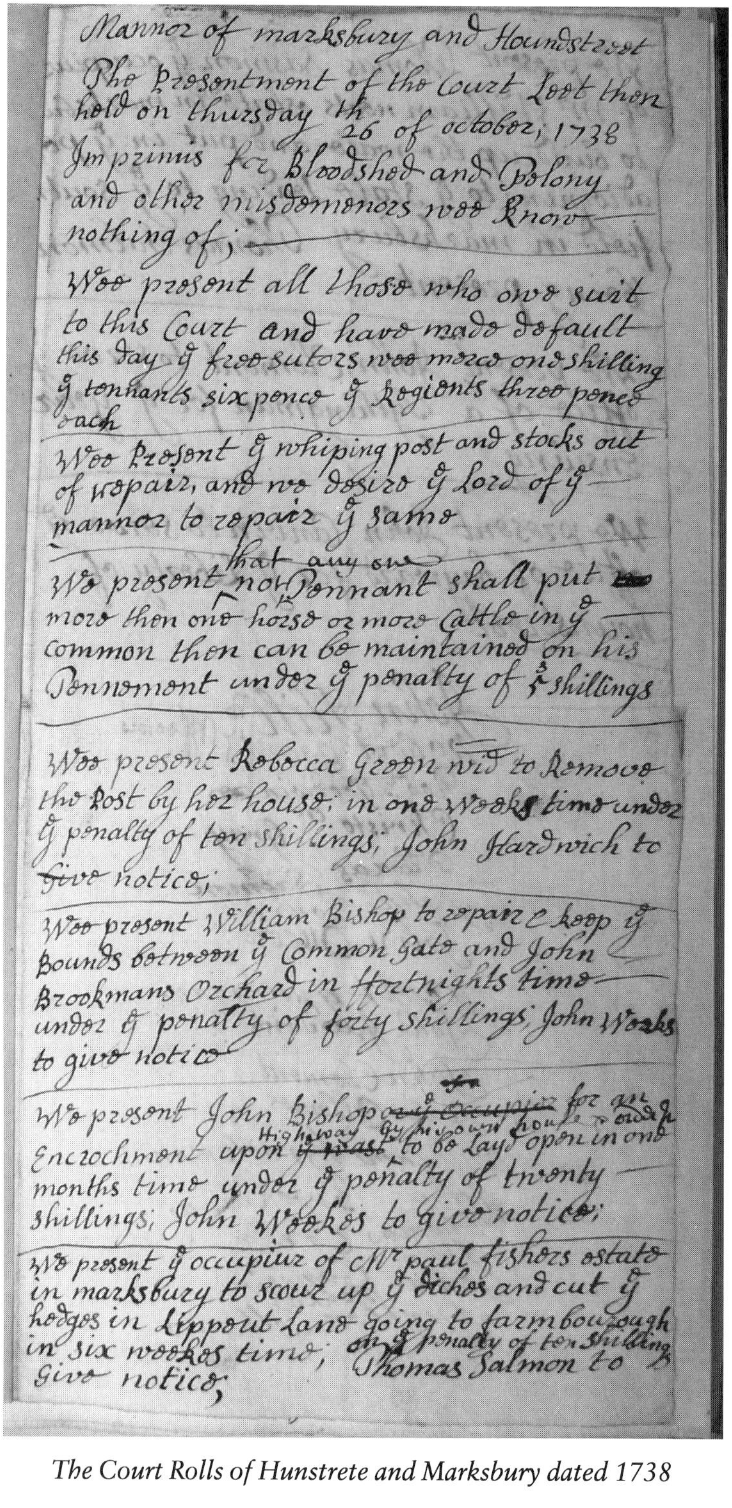

Mannor of marksbury and Houndstreet
The Presentment of the Court Leet then held on thursday 26th of october; 1738
Imprimis for Bloodshed and Felony and other misdemenors wee know nothing of;
Wee present all those who owe suit to this Court and have made default this day ye free sutors wee moree one shilling ye tennants sixpence ye Regidents three pence each
Wee present ye whiping post and stocks out of repair, and we desire ye Lord of ye mannor to repair ye same
We present that any one not Tennant shall put more then one horse or more Cattle in ye common then can be maintained on his Tennement under ye penalty of 5 shillings
Wee present Rebecca Green wid to Remove the Post by her house in one weeks time under ye penalty of ten shillings; John Hardwich to give notice;
Wee present William Bishop to repair & keep ye Bounds between ye Common Gate and John Brookmans Orchard in ffortnights time under ye penalty of forty shillings; John Weeks to give notice
We present John Bishop for an Encrochment upon ye Highway by his own house to be layd open in one months time under ye penalty of twenty shillings; John Weekes to give notice;
We present ye occupiur of Mr paul fishers estate in marksbury to scour up ye diches and cut ye hedges in Leppout Lane going to farmborough in six weekes time, on ye penalty of ten shillings Thomas Salmon to give notice,

The Court Rolls of Hunstrete and Marksbury dated 1738

All tenants were members of the manor court so were said to owe 'Suit of Court', which made attendance compulsory. The names of absentees would be presented to the court, by the reeve, and they would be fined unless they had a valid excuse.

The reeve or hayward would also present to the court any tenant's deaths or the surrender of any tenancies. They would state the extent, the rents and all other obligations attached to the tenancy and whether the 'heriot' had been paid. This was an early form of death duty and was normally the best beast, often a draught ox or cow. This later reverted to a monetary payment. Usually the family heir would then claim tenancy by 'custom of the manor' and be awarded it by right of inheritance on payment of a 'fine' or entrance fee.

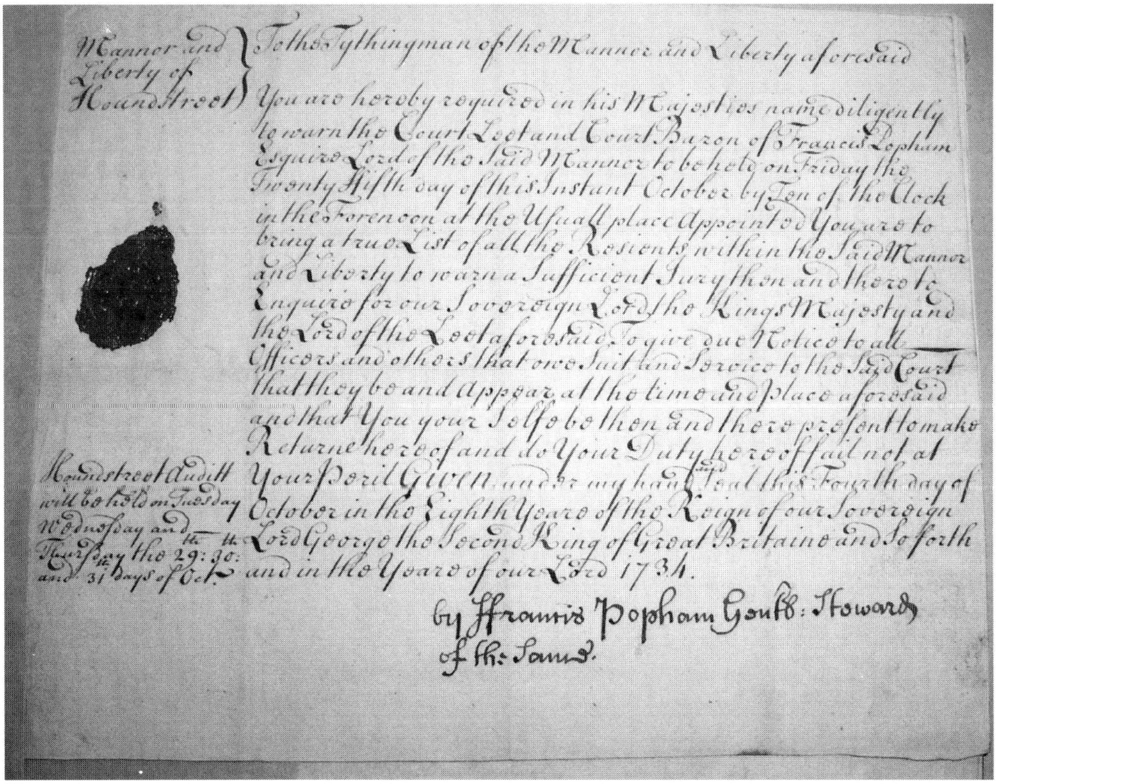

Mannor and Liberty of Houndstreet } To the Tythingman of the Mannor and Liberty aforesaid

You are hereby required in his Majesties name diligently to warn the Court Leet and Court Baron of Francis Popham Esquire Lord of the Said Mannor to be held on Friday the Twenty Fifth day of this Instant October by Ten of the Clock in the Forenoon at the Usuall place Appointed You are to bring a true List of all the Resients within the Said Mannor and Liberty to warn a Sufficient Jury then and there to Enquire for our Sovereign Lord the Kings Majesty and the Lord of the Leet aforesaid To give due Notice to all Officers and others that owe Suit and Service to the Said Court that they be and Appear at the time and place aforesaid and that You your Selfe be then and there present to make Returne hereof and do Your Duty hereof faile not at Your Peril Given under my hand and Seal this Fourth day of October in the Eighth Yeare of the Reign of our Sovereign Lord George the Second King of Great Britaine and So forth and in the Yeare of our Lord 1734.

by ffrancis Popham Gent: Steward of the Same.

Houndstreet Audit will be held on Tuesday Wednesday and Thursday the 29: 30: and 31 days of Oct.

Document requiring the tythingman, or elected representative, to ensure court attendance by tenants

Offences were then presented including negligent maintenance of buildings, trespass, damage to property, altering boundaries and illegal activities such as cutting timber or poaching. An appropriate penalty would then be imposed. The 'custom of the manor,' as remembered down the generations, established the force of law in that manor.

Normally reeves or haywards would be appointed annually from among the tenants, although one individual of family could hold the post for a number of years.

Examples taken from the Marksbury and Hunstrete court rolls make fascinating reading and give a detailed insight into the trials and tribulations of everyday life. I have selected just a few from the many available, which record transgressions by lord and tenant alike!

1726 *Mr Francis Popham esquire to mend the pound of Hunstrete in a months time*

1727 *Mr Francis Popham to mend the footpath*

John Collins for an encroachment on the common

1728 *John Collins again*

The pound again

1729 *John Bishop for continued encroachment against the Hoult gate*

1731 *The common pound and whipping post out of repair*

No tenant can stock on the common more than one horse and as many cattle as they can maintain on the tenement

1732 *Ye pound and whipping post and stocks to be out of repair*

Ye house that Mirah Brown lived in to be out of repair

1763 *We present William Palmer to be taken tenant for the late Collings*

1793 *We present that if any strange beast comes into this manor and is not claimed within one year and one day it belongs to the Lady of the Manor as an estray agreeable to the ancient custom of the said manor*

The above also indicate the main forms of punishment for petty offences, apart from fines. Most parishes had a whipping post, with this used mainly for women. Stocks had been a deterrent since Saxon times. In 1405 an act was passed stating that they had to be provided by law, but this had lapsed by the 1830's. They were used for blasphemy, drunkenness, breaking the Sabbath and so on.

The court also heard a report from the hayward on strays impounded and received the fines he had collected. It then publicly 'proclaimed' any animals whose owners had not been traced. Tenants had a year and a day to claim them before they became the property of the Lord.

The income from fines proved to be a considerable source of revenue for the estate, although it varied somewhat, as the following examples from the account records show

1820 £ 2 7s 0d

1825 £16 19s 6d

1830 £ 1 19s 0d

According to the Park Book the strays included: horses, cattle, pigs, sheep, asses, lambs and calves. The pound was a small enclosure in the area where the telephone box is now. The area of grass adjacent to this is known as the village green and it is likely that the stocks and whipping post were here, this being a central location.

There was a system of game preservation and estate management bonds from 1730 – 1802 (see chapter on Gamekeeping).

It would seem that the manorial courts were replaced, by magistrates' courts, in the early part of the 19th century. The last reference to a court at Hunstrete that I can find is

1826 Expenses at Houndstreet Court

Account books of the 19th century detail various convictions for poaching, trespass and theft, which were dealt with at the local magistrates' court. Examples include

1817 By expenses at justice meeting convicting Thos. Bacon in penalty of £0 5s 0d and costs for cutting an ash sapling and Roger Windmill in penalty of £5 0s 0d and costs in setting rabbit wires in Houndstreet Park. Windmill being unable to pay the fine was committed to prison. By a reward to Richard Love for convicting Thos. Bacon of cutting an ash sapling

1831 By Mr Simmons for committing Thos Hanney to prison for fishing £0 6s 6d

Although the manorial courts no longer took place, the Popham family continued to serve the community in matters of law and order. In the first part of the 20th century Hugh Leyborne Popham was chairman of the magistrates at Keynsham Court and his granddaughter Beatrice was sworn in on the same bench in 1989. She continues to fulfil this role and is a member of the Avon and Somerset Police Authority.

Daily Life

The Popham papers provide a unique record of the minutia of everyday life throughout the three and a half centuries they occupied Hunstrete, when it was not let. The detail is variable, as is the amount and type of documentary evidence, the most prolific being that of the 19th century. The various records make for interesting reading and supply a wealth of information down the centuries.

Household Matters

The earliest material is from 1646 with the inventory of the estate compiled on the death of Francis Popham. This gives a detailed picture of the house itself, with a room by room description, together with a comprehensive list of contents (for full account see appendix 3). It describes furniture, carpets, curtains, cushions, wall hangings and bedding, together with the contents of the kitchen, the wash house and the brew house, plus linen, pewter and books. It also lists the coach with two horses to pull it, the market mare, two coal horses, saddles and other horse furniture and six swine!

Other documentary evidence from the 17th century is limited and often difficult to read. One of the few that I can decipher is for the purchase of needles and park thread and also hops in 1649. The accounts also record that in1673 the chimney man swept the chimneys at Houndstreet House, the New Lodge, the Baker's House, Woodborough Farm House and the Old Lodge.

By the 18th century the records are easier to interpret but still somewhat sparse. In 1702 a lease provides snippets of information such as pigs and poultry were kept, as were oxen, and that there was a still house for brewing. Storage facilities for wood and coal used in the household are also mentioned. Maintenance bills include painting and repairs to the buildings, the windows and the guttering. There are payments for door and gate locks, a padlock for the coach house and 32 sacks of coal.

Other household purchases include cleaning materials, a brass kettle and various items for the dairy, these being a cheese tub and stand, a lead for a cheese press, cheese tongs and a barrel churn. In 1734 a Mr Hunter received payment for Keynsham cakes. These were named after a nearby town but what they were I have been unable to discover. In the same year there are also payments to the butcher and for white wine.

Alcohol played an important role with payments for malt and hops, hogsheads for beer, apples for cider and glass bottles. There is a bill for cooperage that I assume to be for the making of barrels to store the beer and cider in. By 1772 there is a wine account in a separate book. It specifically mentions claret and burgundy from Houndstreet of which there were 43 in the cellar together with beer and ale,

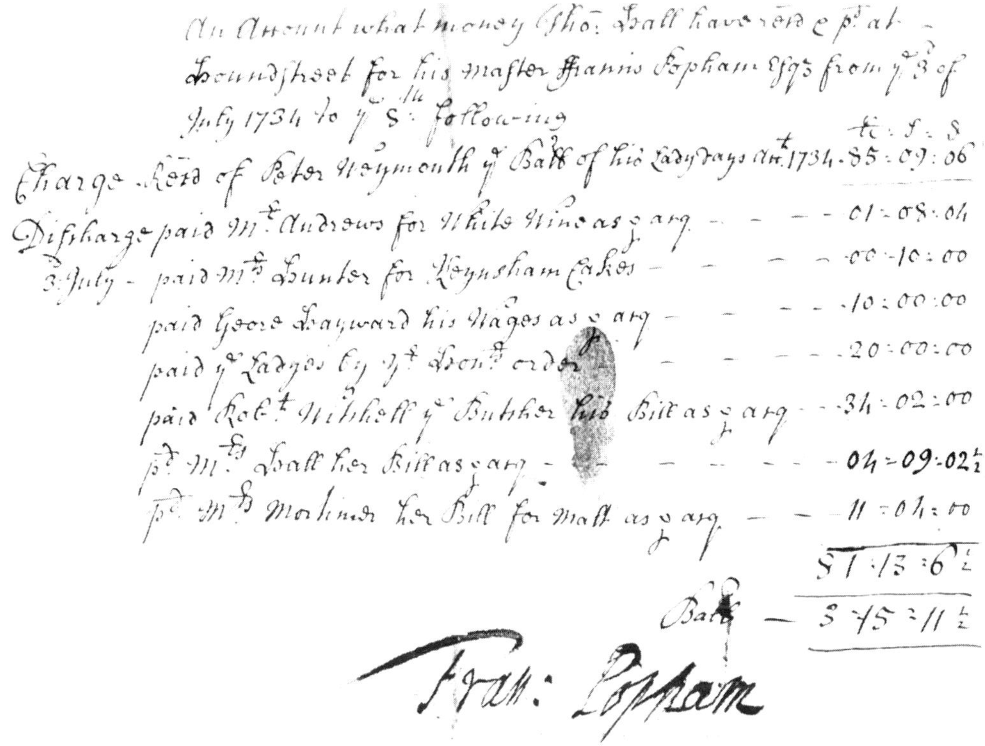

An Account what money Tho: Ball have recd & pd at Houndstreet for his master Francis Popham Esqr from ye 3 of July 1734 to ye 8th following

		£ : s : d
Charge	recd of Peter Weymouth ye Ball of his Lady days Acct 1734	85 : 09 : 06
Discharge	paid Mr Andrews for White Wine as p acq	01 : 08 : 04
3 July	paid Mrs Hunter for Keynsham Cakes	00 : 10 : 00
	paid George Hayward his Wages as p acq	10 : 00 : 00
	paid ye Ladyes by ye Docrs order	20 : 00 : 00
	paid Robt Mitchell ye Butcher his Bill as p acq	34 : 02 : 00
	pd Mrs Ball her Bill as p acq	04 : 09 : 02½
	pd Mrs [illegible] her Bill for malt as p acq	11 : 04 : 00
		81 : 13 : 6½
	Ball	3 : 15 : 11½

Fran: Popham

Extract from the account book of 1734 showing payment for Keynsham cakes

madeira, port, perry, white wine and sweet wine. It records the dates when guests dined at Hunstrete and the wines served, alcohol consumed by the family, port given as gifts and a weekly supply of port to the cook. Similarly by 1773 the butcher's accounts appear independently. The household consumed large quantities of meat with orders being placed for between 6lb and 154lb every few days, mostly for beef.

The records for the 19th century are far more comprehensive and provide further detail about the day to day household of the Pophams. Food purchases include biscuits, currants for jelly, fruit, preserved ginger, Bath buns, lobster, guinea fowl, oysters, apricot marmalade, orange marmalade and raspberry jam. They also sent Cheddar cheese and butter to Littlecote and recorded payment for several other waggon trips to here, presumably carrying goods from one to the other.

Household purchases included candles, mops, brooms and malt and hops to brew beer for haymaking. Bills for the animals show the purchase of dogsmeat, oats for the coach and saddle horses and carthorses and payment to the blacksmith. Improvements included a replacement kitchen range with a smokejack firescreen, the purchase of new chairs and the painting of the salon, with the oil, turpentine and colours being included in the bill.

That the Pophams took care of their health is evident. They were paid up members of the Bath hospital and settled a bill for medicines from the surgeon in 1809. In 1823 General Popham subscribed to the Bath Dispensary, the General Hospital, and the Casualty Hospital, obviously to cover all eventualities!

By the twentieth century the meticulous recording of previous times had ceased, making the task of studying everyday life much more difficult.

Social Life

We are able to glean much about the Pophams social life from a range of sources. Writing in his diary, John Harington MP of Kelston Park, near Bath, tells of various visits to Hunstrete both for business and pleasure. Entries for 1646 include

> *Tuesday 23 June*
>
> *I dine at Hunstert. Mr Edward Popham took the oaths of a Justice of peace.*
>
> *Munday 29 June*
>
> *Come to Hunstert. Mr Alexander Popham defer taking the oaths. He and his brother journey for London. He commend Mr Henly, complain of Sir John Horners unkindness, also expres himself of his wife, of his Mothers chaplen, etc. very religiously per omnia.*
>
> *Munday 7 September*
>
> *Go to Sir Rowland Wainsford. Speak with Mr Alexander Popham*

In 1653 he writes

> *Friday 15th July*
>
> *Mr Thomas and I to Hunster. Mr Aldworth, Mr Greenfield, Mr Thomas etc. there. Colonel Popham and wife from whome.*

The Pophams were involved in the law and politics throughout the centuries, often serving as JP's and MP's. Further evidence of their social influence and political role in the 19th century is shown in the accounts by the purchase of 51 votes in 1807 for Gore Langton, their near neighbour, residing at Newton Park.

That they maintained an active social life is underlined by an order for an engraving plate for cards and a pack of visiting cards. The wine book of 1772 - 1774 also records when guests came to dine, which was frequently. Hunstrete House had a bowling green, as the schedule for the 1759 estate map shows, no doubt used by both the family and their guests. The Grand Mansion was also built with entertainment in mind, with its closeness to Georgian Bath, a distinct social advantage. The Pophams, according to the household accounts, purchased a billiard table together with a green cloth for it in 1790 and cues with lacquered brass handles in 1792.

In the 18th century they subscribed to the Pump Rooms at Bath, this being the meeting place of high society at that time. The Day Book of 1806 - 1807 shows they purchased play tickets at £1 0s 0d each and reserved their seats for an extra 1s 0d and also treated the servants to 6s 0d seats. This was presumably for the newly opened Theatre Royal at Bath. In 1824 there is a payment of £2 2s 0d for opera glasses for Edward Popham. That they enjoyed music is indicated by a bill for the repair of the harp in 1806. On 20th October 1828 the Pophams paid £1 0s 0d on each occasion for the bells to be rung at Marksbury, Publow and Pensford churches to celebrate the coming of age of their son William.

That the family were keen hunters is apparent by the stag's head used as the family crest and on their coat of arms. This may well have been the reason why Sir John acquired the estate in the 17th century, being aware of its long association with the sport. A solid gold button found in the garden of number 5 Hunstrete has a hound motif and may well have come from a hunting jacket or a gamekeeper's coat.

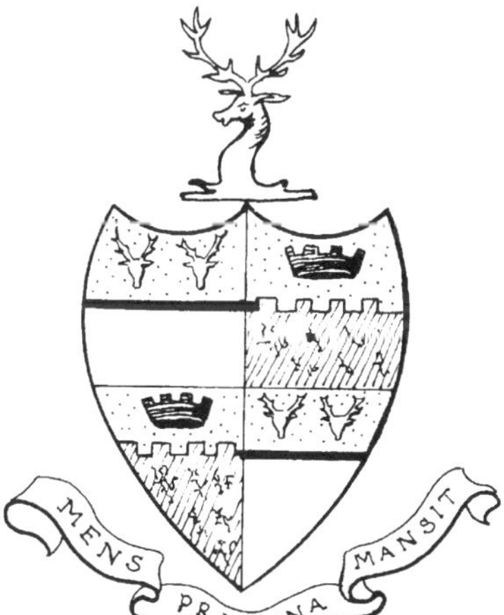

Leyborne Popham family Coat of Arms

Motto The former mind remains

The Popham family crest

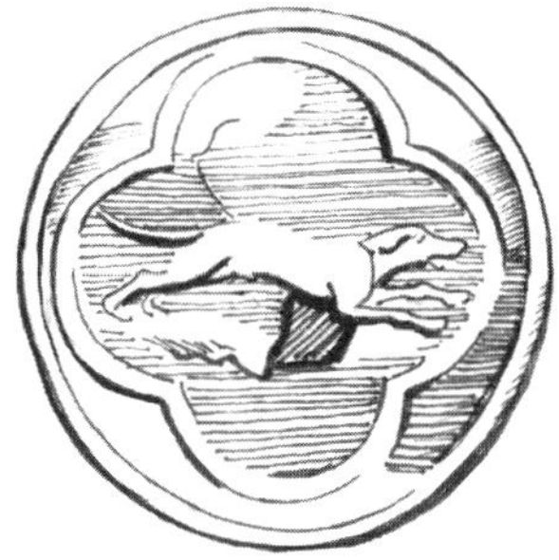

Gold livery button

Further evidence comes from an account entry for 1706 which records

A medison for the hounds being bit by a mad dog

52 bushels of malt and grain brewed against hunting the deer

Subsequent to this there is a lack of documentary evidence, as to their continued involvement in hunting, apart a from a bond for poaching in 1754 when a male deer was killed out of the park and a note on the cost of hampers for venison in 1811. However the tradition obviously continued with Mrs Leyborne Buller Popham being Master of the Mendip Hunt in the early 1950's.

Shooting gradually became more popular than hunting and Hunstrete provided this for the Littlecote estate. The house is listed as the Lodge in the 1843 Tithe Map schedule and an 1891 inventory includes a gunroom leading to the stable yard. This is now an office off the private dining room.

Shooting party c. 1938. Hugh Leyborne Popham third left and Elizabeth Leyborne Popham front right

There were regular shoots in the first half of the 20th century with birthdays in particular being celebrated in this way. H.G. Popham was a particularly keen exponent and participated regularly both locally and abroad. The game record book from the early part of the 20th century makes for interesting reading.

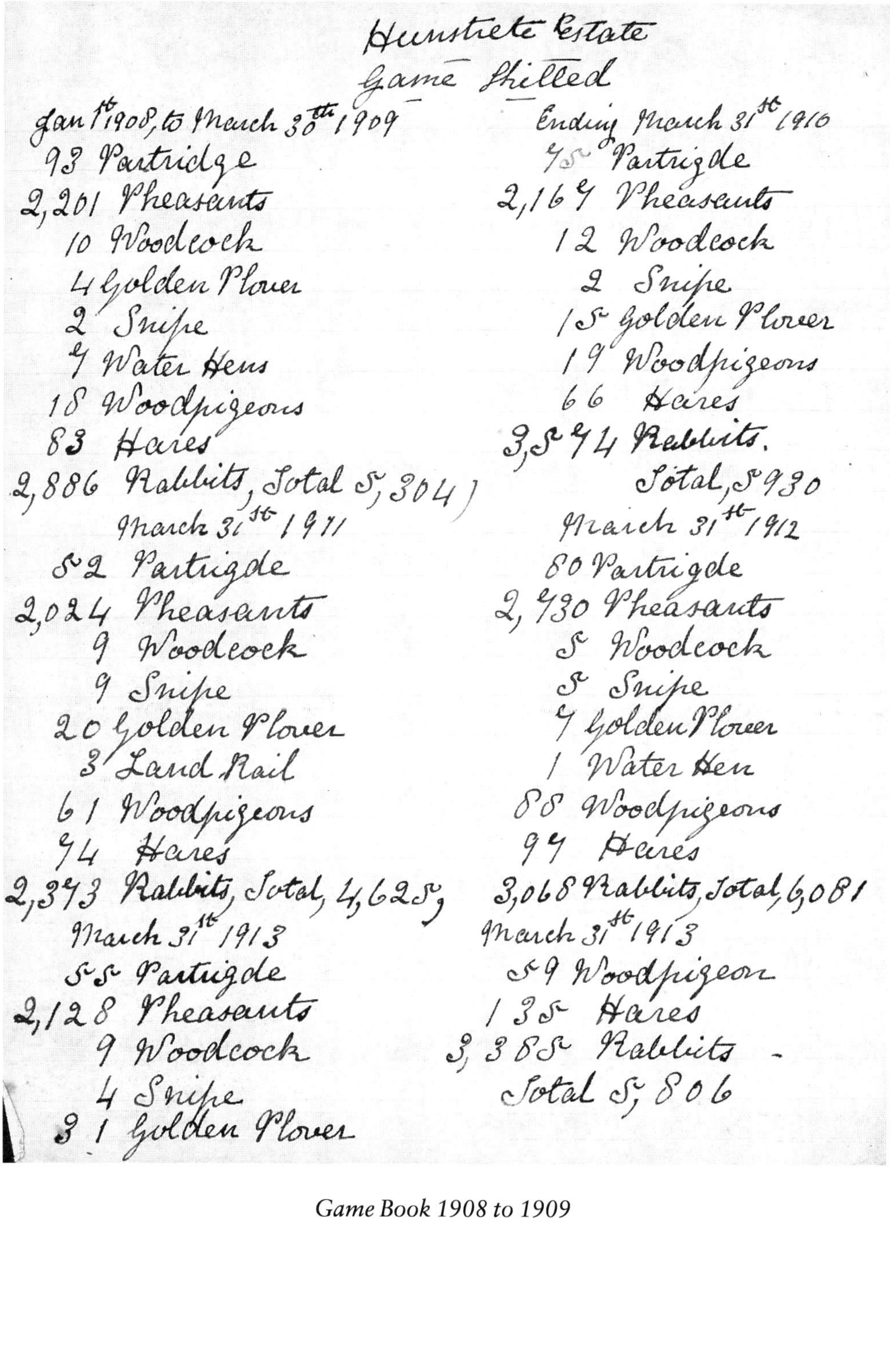

Hunstrete Estate

Game Killed

Jan 1st 1908, to March 30th 1909
93 Partridge
2,201 Pheasants
10 Woodcock
4 Golden Plover
2 Snipe
7 Water Hens
18 Woodpigeons
83 Hares
2,886 Rabbits, Total 5,304)

Ending March 31st 1910
75 Partigde
2,167 Pheasants
12 Woodcock
2 Snipe
15 Golden Plover
19 Woodpigeons
66 Hares
3,574 Rabbits.
Total, 5930

March 31st 1911
52 Partigde
2,024 Pheasants
9 Woodcock
9 Snipe
20 Golden Plover
3 Land Rail
61 Woodpigeons
74 Hares
2,373 Rabbits, Total, 4,625,

March 31st 1912
80 Partigde
2,730 Pheasants
5 Woodcock
5 Snipe
7 Golden Plover
1 Water Hen
88 Woodpigeons
97 Hares
3,068 Rabbits, Total, 6,081

March 31st 1913
55 Partigde
2,128 Pheasants
9 Woodcock
4 Snipe
31 Golden Plover

March 31st 1913
59 Woodpigeon
135 Hares
3,385 Rabbits
Total 5,806

Game Book 1908 to 1909

Education

Generations of the Popham family attended public schools, traditionally followed by Oxford University. They were well read with subscriptions to the Bath Herald and to the library. They also corresponded regularly there being numerous letters among the Popham papers. In 1758 there is a note from Francis Popham to his wife, written whilst in London. It is fascinating to read, particularly the reference to the children being at school.

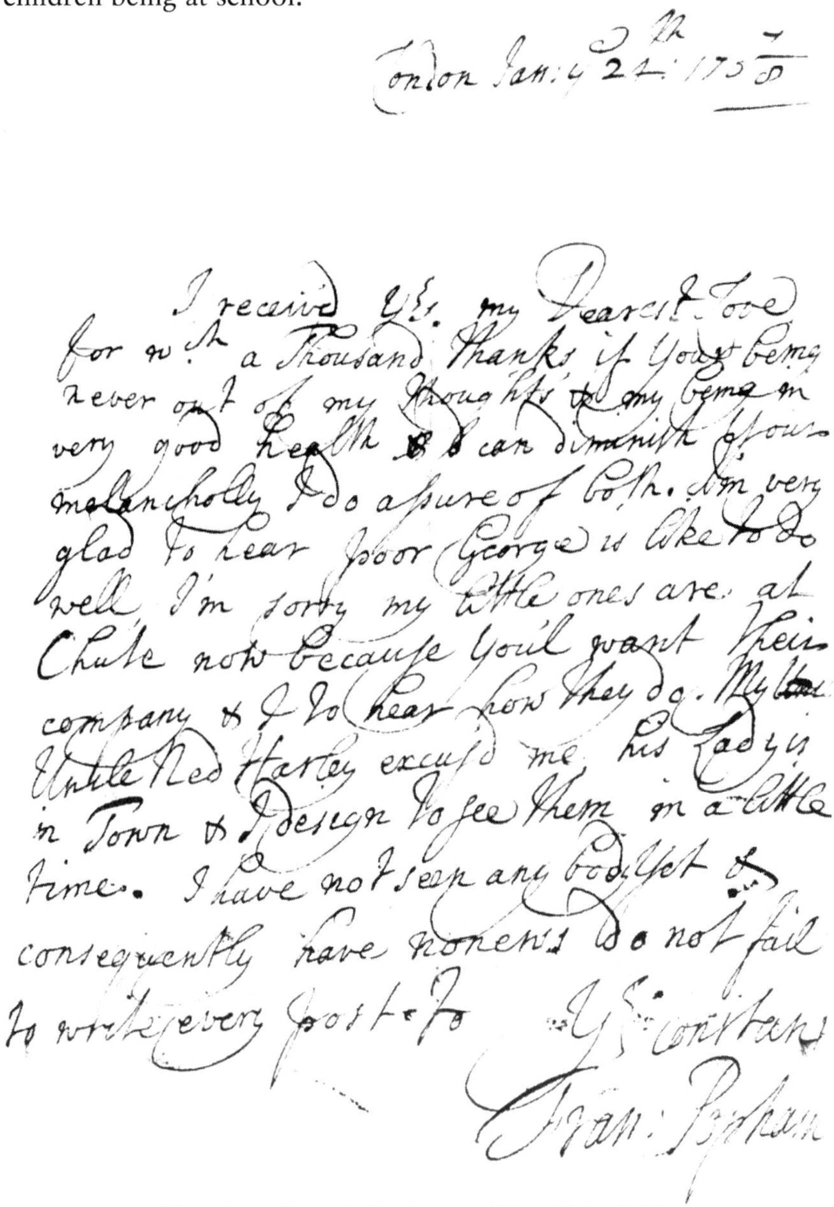

London Jan:y 21th: 1758

I receiv'd Y.rs my Dearest Love for w.ch a Thousand Thanks if Your being never out of my Thoughts & my being in very good health & I can diminish your melancholly I do assure of both. I'm very glad to hear poor George is like to do well. I'm sorry my little ones are at Chute now because you'll want their company & I to hear how they do. My Uncle Ned Harley excus'd me his Lady is in Town & I design to see them in a little time. I have not seen any body yet & consequently have no news do not fail to write every post to Y.rs constant

Fran: Popham

Note from Francis Popham to his wife in 1758

There is also mention, in 1771, of two letters from Mr Popham to a person called Adams. The first refers to the former's illness, whilst the second concerns a monetary matter. In 1782 Daniel Green, Dorothy Popham's steward, wrote to her about progress on the building of the Grand Mansion.

The Day Book of 1806 - 1807 record payments for writing paper and permanent ink and for letters and postage, including a Christmas box for the letter boy.

Travel

There are frequent references in the records to travel. In 1673 there is a bill for a journey to Littlecote, a trend that continued for centuries, with the accounts recording numerous trips to and from here. There is also a payment in 1807 for the hire of a coach to and from London. In 1809 the Pophams paid for the cost of a waggon to Bristol and a year's subscription to the Well's turnpike, the latter being a regular expenditure.

Philanthropy

That the Pophams were aware of their role as benefactors from early on is evident from an audit of 1649 - 1650 which records a payment to the poor of Marksbury of 3s 0d. Later charitable payments included donations to the Pensford Friendly society, the Publow clubs and to a man hurt by a bull! In 1814 they gave money to the poor of Pensford to be distributed as bread and in 1826 there is a record of the annual allowance to Hunstrete poor, this being for the sum of £20 0s 0d.

General Popham subscribed to Marksbury School in 1822 and Bath Penitentiary in 1823. He also provided an annual dinner for his tenants, the bill for which in 1823 came to £6 15s 0d. The 1883 - 1884 Labour and Wages book reveals that he paid his workers when they were ill and for Christmas Day, this being their only day off in the year.

In the early part of the 20th century Mrs Popham visited each cottage in Hunstrete, around Christmas time, bearing gifts for each member of the family. Tony Gill told me that she took a lot of trouble in choosing the presents and that they were always well received. He recalled his grandmother making the house presentable before the visit and putting on her 'posh' voice and best manners for the occasion.

Whenever I talked to the older people in the area they recalled the Pophams with affection and told me that they were widely regarded as good employers. They also referred to them as being of the 'old school' in terms of how they treated the villagers and their staff.

Elizabeth Lloyd (nee Leyborne Popham)

Elizabeth Lloyd was born at Hunstrete in 1909. She was the eldest daughter of Hugh Leyborne Popham and his wife Janet and had two younger sisters, Mary and Ann. She lived in the family home, apart from a spell at boarding school at Sandicote in Dorset, until she left to get married in 1939. Her parents had married in 1908 and her father decided to let Littlecote and take his new wife to Hunstrete. Here the family led what Elizabeth described as a simple life as her father didn't particularly like socialising.

He bred dogs, mainly wire haired terriers, which he enjoyed showing and often won prizes. He also kept Jersey cattle, being one of the first people in the country to stock the breed and also exhibited them. His wife bred chickens and entered them in poultry shows. Elizabeth recalled them being washed and starched in the laundry prior to such events. Her mother had an extensive rose garden and was a keen needlewoman.

As young children the girls had both a nanny and a governess. Elizabeth recalled other staff including the Baileys of Woollard with Florence being the parlourmaid and Maud the housemaid, Madge Treeby the ladies' maid and Mrs Kirkaldy the cook. The latter was with the family throughout their time in the house and was affectionately known as 'Cuckoo' from her habit of putting her head round doors and calling out the greeting. There was also Rawlings the gamekeeper.

Fir Tree Villa being moved into place c. 1938

The children amused themselves around the estate often riding their bikes through the grounds. They swam in the lake having a springboard at one end for diving. They sailed on it in the summer using a dingy belonging to Ann and skated on it when conditions permitted during the winter. Elizabeth particularly recalled the time when the lake froze over for six weeks in 1917. At this time there were no trees around the perimeter and her father kept a collection of ornamental ducks on it. They also used to play in the chicken house until they caught fleas! Their parents then purchased a shed for the purpose, about 1938, that the children christened 'Fir Tree Villa.'

The family kept a boat at Falmouth and sailed during the summer. In the winter they skied in Austria and Switzerland. Although recalling a happy childhood Elizabeth also remembers feeling isolated and lonely at Hunstrete, as she was six years older than her next sister. She told me that it was very cold in the winter, as the only source of heating was open fires. She and her sisters often got dressed in the large walk in airing cupboard, this being the warmest room in the house.

As she grew older she developed a love of cars and often acted as the family chauffeur. She was presented at court and soon became embroiled in something of a social whirl. There was the usual calendar of events for debutantes plus outings and occasions based at Hunstrete. The estate was maintained for game and there were regular shoots together with special birthday shooting parties. Her father kept a game book that shows he shot at other estates in the area and that he regularly went to Holland after duck.

Aston Martins c.1936. Elizabeth Leyborne Popham is driving the car on the right

From an early age Elizabeth kept a photographic record and also compiled what she called her 'cuttings books'. These have provided a fascinating account of her life at Hunstrete and beyond and together with her father's photographic collection give a fascinating insight into the estate in the first part of the 20th century. As she looked through them her recall of events was both detailed and fascinating. She told me that the French windows in the bar were originally a main entrance to the house and that the stairs used to go up from here, information she had been told by her father which probably refers to the alterations of 1890. Her parent's bedroom was the room now called 'Dove' and it wasn't until she stayed there when it was a hotel in the 1990's that she entered this for the first time!

Elizabeth was married from Hunstrete in 1939 and went to live in Essex. She told me that the family sold Littlecote in 1929 to the Wills family of Bristol, but retained Hunstrete. On her father's death in 1943 it passed to the Buller family, due to an arrangement made by her grandfather to relieve his financial difficulties. They added Leyborne Popham to their name, there being a distant connection. His wife then moved into Hunstrete cottage, which was formerly the land agent's house. This has remained in the family ensuring a continuing link between the Pophams and Hunstrete despite the eventual sale of the estate.

Florence Bates (nee Bates)

Florence was sixteen when she went to work at Hunstrete House in 1909. She took up the post of between maid, having already been 'in service' for two years in Bath. At that time there were four other women employed by the household beside herself. These were the housekeeper cum cook, the parlour maid, the house maid and the laundry maid. A month after Florence was taken on, Mrs Popham gave birth to Elizabeth, her eldest daughter, so a nursemaid was added to the staff.

The between maid shared a room with the laundry maid and was the earliest of the household to rise. Her first task of the day was to light the range and get the kettle boiling before the parlour maid came to make the maids' tea. This had a back boiler and two ovens, one for roasting and one for baking, the latter having a glass door.

Every morning, she worked for about an hour and a half helping the housemaid upstairs. The remainder of her day was spent assisting the cook, whom Florence regarded as very fussy. She was particularly so about carrots which had to be pared thinly until 'you could see the pink'. These were then finely chopped and added to the soup for dinner.

Florence recalled that washing up was done with soda in the big lead sink, with its two taps. This was a great luxury compared with the cottages in the village. The plates had to be carefully dried, rather than left to drain on the wooden rack. Her other duties included cleaning the kitchen, larder and servants' hall. On a normal day she would be busy from 6 o'clock in the morning until 10 o'clock at night.

Amongst other household staff she remembered was a boy employed to fetch the milk from the Home Farm, bring in wood and coal, clean boots and lead the pony that pulled the lawn mower! There were also two gardeners and a poultry boy. Hugh Leyborne Popham exhibited Brahma fowls and it was the task of this lad to prepare the birds. He had to wash and try them in the laundry room and then carefully guard them, in baskets in the kitchen, until it was time for the show.

On Sundays the maids were required to walk to church at Marksbury, whatever the weather, whilst the Squire and his wife went by car. On alternate Sundays they were permitted to go home for the afternoon and evening. The between maid had an afternoon off on Thursdays, although this often amounted to no more than a couple of hours, as she had to be back to help with the evening meal. Once a month Florence went into the study to receive her wages from Mrs Popham, totalling £8 a year.

Madge Treeby (nee Lewis)

Madge went to work at Hunstrete from 1929, when she was 15 years old, until 1935. She was employed as a seamstress and did all the family's sewing. She recalls darning stockings, making clothes, repairing linen by sewing the sides to the middle and sewing the chiffon onto Mary's train when she was presented at Court.

She also had to take out Ann, the youngest child, every afternoon following her morning lessons. She was expected to help with the spring cleaning when the Pophams were away. Madge started work at 7.30am and was on call until 10.00pm. She had half a day off every week and every other

Sunday afternoon and evening. On the alternate Sundays she was free until 1.00pm. She started on a wage of about £15 a year, which eventually rose to £18.

Her days were very similar. At 7.30am she had breakfast with the staff, worked until lunchtime and then continued until she was off duty. The estate employees, most of who lived in, were well fed eating the same meals as the family. They particularly enjoyed milk, cream and home made butter from the Jersey herd. They were also well treated and when Madge got married Mrs Popham sent the Daimler, complete with chauffeur, to take her to chapel. The other employees she can name were:

Flo Bailey - the parlourmaid who answered the door, waited at table and cleaned the silver.

Doris Smith - the housemaid who told her about the job and with whom she shared her time off. She did the cleaning and was very thorough.

Mrs Kirkaldy - the cook

Peggy Primrose - the kitchen maid

Jesse Palmer - the head gardener

Jack Parsons - the undergardener

Ern Barnes - the assistant gardener

Les Barnes - the kennel man who was in charge of the pedigree terriers which were shown.

Victor Hunt - the chauffeur

Mr Deacon - who kept an eye on the estate. His wife and sister came in three times a week to do the laundry for the family and staff.

Trussler- the gamekeeper who had to place two rabbits every day in an outside box to feed the two Pekinese and the cat.

Madge can recall the polished oak main staircase and the panelled hall, both now painted, and the black leaded range being changed for an Aga. She remembers life at Hunstrete as 'Like living in a convent.' It was quiet and unexciting so the staff had to make their own fun such as practical jokes. On one occasion the carpets were rolled up for spring cleaning. Madge crawled inside one and when Ern and Jack came to move it they couldn't understand why it was so heavy. When they discovered her they chased her down the back stairs and up the front ones with much ensuing hilarity.

On another occasion Ern persuaded her, one evening, to borrow a pair of the childrens' skates and have a go on the frozen lake whilst the family were engaged in their evening meal. She did this and was so engrossed that she completely forgot the time. She ran back and tried to sneak in the pantry window. With her head inside and legs and bottom outside, she was tipped the wink that Mrs Popham was coming along the corridor! She dropped back down and tried again later, fortunately getting away with it! Even after all these years Madge still feels guilty about this!!!

After she left their employ Madge retained links with the family and went back to assist at the weddings of both Mary and subsequently Elizabeth. They, in turn, have fond memories of her and refer to her with warmth.

Anne Stachowski (nee de Bruyne)

When the Germans invaded Holland on 10th May 1940, Anne's father was the British vice counsel in Flushing. The family already had plans in hand to evacuate, should this happen, and duly left for England. Ann aged 16, her 11 year old brother and her parents drove through Belgium and France, before embarking on an empty troop ship at Le Havre, to cross the channel to Southampton. Anne's father then telephoned Hugh Leyborne Popham who invited them to stay at Hunstrete. He was an old family friend and used to visit Holland to shoot ducks with her father.

They arrived at the house on 20th May 1940 and were confined to movement within five miles of Hunstrete as they were foreigners. They found it in a pre war state. Anne recalls various members of staff including Old Deacon and Dick Palmer, the woodsmen, who used to come to the back of the house, where huge barrels of cider were stored in a barn, and fill their jugs before work. There was also Mr Himmens who ran Park Farm assisted by Rosewell and Edgar Smith. Ern Barnes and three boys maintained the garden, which was famous for its roses. Jack Parsons looked after the wire haired fox terriers and Brahma chickens. Others included Trussler the gamekeeper, Hunt the chauffeur, Fred Primrose the butler, his wife Peggy who helped in the kitchen and two laundry maids who worked in a room above the stables, which at that time were used as a garage.

She told me about a number of incidents that happened whilst she was at Hunstrete including Hugh Popham shooting rats in the hen runs. Also the time when the onions that the gardener, Ern Barnes, sowed had just come up and Mrs Popham, who liked to help, hoed them off thinking that they were weeds. She also has many memories connected with the game on the estate. Much of this would be taken to Bath and she would go with the Pophams, and have coffee in Fortes, whilst it was being delivered to the shops. That used for home consumption would be hung in a cage, to protect it, until it was considered ready to eat. She tells of Peggy Parsons skimming maggots out of the gravy, made from pheasant juices, before it was served at table!

Anne spent a lot of her time with the Popham children. She remembers swimming in the lake with Ann and diving from a board situated near the cottages. In winter she put everyone else to shame by skating on one leg backwards, having learnt to do so in her native Holland. She used to groom the Pekinese dogs, Bambo and Twinky. They were long haired and consequently their coats got very matted. When they saw Anne advancing towards them, comb in hand, they would run up one staircase and down the other! She also rode her horse from Hunstrete to Bath when she needed a new saddle, taking it right into the shop, which was near Kingsmead Square.

In September 1940 Anne's father was sent to Fleetwood, to negotiate with Dutch fishermen about working for the British Government, and the family moved there until 1944. Anne came back to Hunstrete at that time, although Mr Popham had died in 1942 and his wife had moved into Hunstrete Cottage. She worked as a land girl for Fred Alward who was now running Park Farm, living in at the farmhouse, and milking the Jersey herd.

Other things Anne remembers are that Hunstrete House and village was supplied with electricity by generators maintained by Ern Barnes, walking across the fields to church at Chelwood on a Sunday and the occasion when a bomb knocked out all the windows of the house. This was one of three that fell on the estate during the Second World War, but damage was minimal.

Anne stayed at Hunstrete for a year, until she joined the Dutch Wrens in London in 1945.

Hunstrete has played a role in war several times during its history. Under the mediaeval system of tenure the manor was required to supply men and arms for the crown in time of conflict. In 1539, Marksbury, which included Hunstrete, had to provide 17 able bodied men for the king. In 1568 - 1569 a Certificate of Musters was compiled for the County of Somerset by Hugh Paulet, Maurice Berkley, Raffe Hopton, knightes, and John Horner, Esquier. This consisted of:

> *All the able men as well as horsemen as fote men with theire armour and weapons as also ot the parkes for the bread of mares and horses within the saide county*

For the tithing of Marksbury, it listed the following:

Ablemen

Walter Mersser	*pekeman*	*Richd. More*	*pekeman*
Nichs. Baker	*gonner*	*Nichs. Courte*	*archer*
Jno. Batersby	*billman*	*Rich Lockyere*	*billman*
Thos. Saunders	*archer*	*Thos. Phelps*	*archer*
Nichs. Phelps	*billman*	*Jno. Saunders*	*billman*
Hugh a Price	*archer*	*Rich. Parsons*	*archer*
Wm. James	*billman*	*Robt. Jones*	*billman*

Armor

One tethinge corset furnished, one jack and one bow, one sheaf of arrows.

Pekemen and billmen fought hand to hand with the enemy. Pikes were a spear like device, on an approximately 16 foot long staff. Billhooks were broader, with a hook on the top and mounted on an eight foot staff. The archers would have used longbows and the gonner would have been part of a cannon crew.

The corset was a metal back and breastplate, whilst the jack was a sleeveless quilted jacket, made of cotton, reinforced with pieces of metal sewn inside.

The English Civil War

The Popham family were strong supporters of Oliver Cromwell during the English Civil War, Alexander the son and heir of Sir Francis, being a colonel in the Parliamentary army. As such he made use of Hunstrete during the campaign. The north and east of Somerset supported the Parliamentary cause whilst the south and west were for the King. By the summer of 1642 the Royalists had established a base in the Bishop's Palace at Wells, a situation which the Puritan element of the county could not ignore.

Plans were made with Sir John Horner of Mells and John Ashe of Freshford for a great Roundhead rendezvous at Chewton Mendip. In early August of the same year Popham billeted his men of the Bath regiment in the grounds of the Hunstrete Estate, prior to meeting up with his contemporaries and their troops on the 5th of that month. The neighbours and tenants of Horner joined Popham's professional soldiers, with the contingent numbering some 1 000 men.The sight of such an army camped at Hunstrete must have been a memorable experience.

In 2002 a number of musket balls from the period, were found in the area that is now the orchard and one can imagine the soldiers dropping them in the fervour of preparation for the ensuing battle. Two cannon balls were also recovered some distance away, maybe having been used for a practice session.

The plan of campaign was to march on the city of Wells and drive the Royalists back to the south. Early on the morning of the 5th August Alexander Popham led the troops to join the massive army assembling on an escarpment overlooking Wells. They reached the detailed assembly point by early afternoon and the decision was taken to abstain from battle until the next day, whilst negotiations took place. The army by now numbered some 12 000 men. The 'Bellum Civile' describing Hopton's campaign of 1642 - 44 gives an account of this event

> *August 5th...there were discovered upon the topp of Mendip hill above the Towne great bodies of men, some horse, but the most part foote, with flying coulours and some pieces of iron ordnance which had bene drawen together by Sir Jo: Horner and Mr. Popham and the rest of the Gentlemen of that party out of the south and east lymitt of Somersetshire, and from Bristoll and other parts, according to the relacion of the countrey men before mencioned that were examined by Sir Jo:Stowell, they were judged to bee about ten or 12 thousand men, and it was about one o'clock in the afternoone when they began to appeare.*

It was decided to attempt negotiation before attacking the city and the troops were forced to spend the night in the open. A letter written by Ashe, one of the Somerset committee, from his base at Freshford on 7th August enables us to visualise the scene. His account refers to 40 000 on the Friday

> *Many had no more weapons but their swords...they lay that night upon the hill above Wells, fasting. Sir John Horner and Master Alexander Popham with his two valiant brothers and Sir John Horner's youngest sonne with many others lay all that night in their Armes upon fursebushes in the open fields*

Negotians failed and warning shots were fired from the Mendip plateau to the city below. This ultimately led to the enemy retreating to Sherborne via Glastonbury and Somerton. An account by a captain who supported the Royalist cause was given in a letter written at the time. It reads as follows

We did also make search in the Bishop's house of Bath and Wells and there we found one of the Bishop's Gods, which was the Lady Mary with the babe in her arms, and she was bound up in a linen cloth and laid in a coffin; this we found in the Bishop's closet, and my father doth intend to send it to the Parliament. At Wells we received order from Colonel Fynes to make all haste we could towards Sherborne.

Although most of the Parliamentarian army then dispersed, some soldiers did enter Wells and a minority ransacked the town. They smashed stained glass in the cathedral, looted the Bishop's Palace and paraded through the streets behind a picture of the Virgin Mary held aloft on a pikestaff.

At Sherborne Castle the enemy were ultimately engaged in 1643. In the ensuing battle the Parliamentarians were victorious but Hugh, Alexander's brother lost his life.

The 1646 inventory drawn up two years after the death of Sir Francis Popham lists 21 muskets in the Hall at Hunstrete, which were probably used in the Civil War.

World War I

Hunstrete was largely unaffected by the First World War except for petrol rationing and a shortage of food supplies. The family's Daimler was put up on blocks in the stable for the duration. Mr Hugh Leyborne Popham drove a much more economical Model T Ford and was granted extra petrol to fulfil his duties as a magistrate at Keynsham County Court and the various other administrative offices he was engaged in. His daughter Elizabeth recalls, as a child, being fed copious amounts of prunes and rabbit, which she was always told, was chicken. Also that the nanny to the Leyborne Popham children at this time, used to threaten that the Germans would come and get her if she didn't behave herself.

World War II

During the Second World War Hunstrete again became a base for action, this time hosting the Pensford unit of the AU or Auxillary Units. This was a guerrilla force whose sole mission was sabotage, in enemy occupied territory, should there be a successful German invasion of England. Somerset had the second largest resistance organisation in the country, with nearly 300 men operating out of 50 secret bases. The headquarters of the Pensford Unit was in Common Wood. The purpose built base, about 14 feet by 10 feet, was like an underground Nissen hut, with blast proof walls. It was accessed by ladder, via a disguised manhole cover, and had an escape tunnel at the rear of the building. It was divided into three sections: the toilet where ammunitions and explosives were also kept, the ration store and living quarters complete with army issue camp beds.

The platoon, according to Donald Brown in 'Somerset Versus Hitler', comprised:

Lt. later Capt. William Trussler - estate gamekeeper - Hunstrete
Henry Bailey - lorry driver - Compton Dando
Lewis Crow - Chelwood
Harding - miner - Pensford
Jim Hooper - builder - Bristol
Vic Hooper - his younger brother
Arthur Lovell - Temple Cloud
Edwin Thomas - builder - Keynsham
A farmer - Ston Easton
A builder - Keynsham

Trussler was an ideal choice as a volunteer knowing the land intimately, particularly at night, through his employment as the estate gamekeeper. Local rumour has it that he stored the ammunition for the unit in the icehouse on the estate, apparently before the purpose built base was completed. He would have recruited like minded local men who knew each other well, with each being sworn to secrecy. They operated under the guise of Home Guard units, with members being exempt from national call up. Jim Hooper recalled his time in the AU as follows

> *I lived in Bristol but I'd been courting out in Woollard. I knew the captain and he asked me to join Pensford Unit. He was Captain Trussler, the gamekeeper. They were just digging out their base in the estate woods. I was a builder so I was useful to them.*
>
> *There were about a dozen in the Unit. All the men were in their late 20s, early 30's. I was one of the younger ones, only 17 at the time. We were not in the Home Guard. We had to sit tight, do nothing, get overrun, until they were past us. Then we had to emerge and do whatever we could to slow them down. There was no suggestion that we were going to stop any attack.*

Sometime during World War II a team of about twenty Welsh soldiers visited Hunstrete Lake, very briefly, for exercises and tests with folding boats. It was winter and freezing cold. Locals remember a big sergeant shouting at his men to get things right as they wouldn't fancy a dip in such weather. They packed up and left within hours. On another occasion a squad of US soldiers with masses of equipment, including lorries and jeeps, parked under the trees where the fishing complex car park is now situated. They stayed for a brief respite, to have a meal and a period of relaxation before moving on. Tony Gill, as a thirteen year old on his school holidays, turned up to watch and recalls being fed many welcome tit bits by the chef.

World War II bomb damage to Hunstrete House and grounds

Hunstrete was hit by enemy action on three occasions during the Second World War. Each time Hunstrete House and the village properties escaped serious damage with all the bombs falling in the grounds of the estate. These left deep craters and on one occasion the strength of the blast blew out all the windows of the house. Also a wooden shed, once used to hang game birds, was blown to pieces. No one was hurt during any of these raids.

Gillian Barnes, whose family lived in the gardener's cottage was a baby at the time. Her parents told her that they put her to sleep in a tin bath, as it was easy to carry. When the air raid sirens went off they took the makeshift bed, complete with sleeping baby, to the cellars beneath the main house. On one occasion when a bomb fell, the force of the blast turned Gillian over in the tin bath! It had been a near miss! The courtyards, outside their house, resembled a freshly dug garden, with the soil having been thrown up by the explosion.

The Popham family also provided a temporary home to the de Braune family who had fled enemy action in Holland (for a full account of this see the chapter on Memories).

The American Connection

From the middle of the 16th century colonisation of the coast of North America proved of interest to many wealthy members of British society, Sir John Popham among them. They were eager to exploit the potential resources available in a new country, thereby increasing their wealth, and consequently provided finanical backing.

In 1605 Captain George Waymouth set sail in the 'Archangel' to explore the coast of Maine. The expedition captured two native Indians on a beach to act as guides and lured three others on board ship with promises of gifts. James Rosier, chronicler of the voyage, taught them basic English. On arrival back in England the Indians were given to the backers of the expedition: three to Sir Fernando Gorges, to train as servants, and two to Sir John Popham. The latter used them to help him plan an expedition to the coast of Maine, in order to assess its suitability for colonisation. This duly took place in 1606 with one of the two ships involved being commanded by Captain Thomas Hanham, Sir John's son in law. This returned, although the other was captured by Spaniards, bringing the news that the land was suitable for settlement and with maps of the area compiled by the ship's navigator Martin Pring.

In the same year King James 1 of England granted a charter to the newly established Virginia Company allowing it the right to settle the east coast of North America. There were to be two ventures with the Plymouth Adventurers Company exploring to the north and the London Virginia Company to the south. Whichever established a successful settlement was entitled to claim the land between them. Their respective fortunes were to prove quite diverse.

The Plymouth Company was very much a family affair being backed by Sir John Popham and several of his sons in law and having as its agent in Plymouth his son Sir Francis. They founded the Popham Colony, named after their principal financier, which was ultimately to fail. The London Company's colony of Jamestown, named in honour of the king, went on to achieve fame as the birthplace of modern America. However, but for a twist of fate, things might have turned out very differently.

On 31st May 1607, under the auspices of the Plymouth Company about 100 colonists, men and boys, set sail from that town aboard two ships, the 'Gift of God' and the 'Mary and John'. The expedition was under the leadership of George Popham, who was probably the nephew of Sir John, and Raleigh Gilbert, a distant relation of Sir Walter Raleigh. Some ten weeks later, on 19th August, they made landfall on a site where the Sagadahoc (Kennebec) river enters the Atlantic, in present day Maine.

On the headland known as Sabino Point, within the modern community of Popham Beach, they constructed 'Fort St. George' naming it after their elected leader.

They erected sufficient buildings to house the 45 people who choose to remain for the winter. The majority of the colonists then returned to England, due to a shortage of food, in October and December of that year.

Despite the harshness of the winter the colony thrived, establishing a fur trade with the Indians and harvesting sarsaparilla root for sale in England as a medicinal plant. However hopes of mining gold were to prove unattainable. In February 1608 the quiet unassuming George Popham died, aged probably about 55, and the more ambitious, adventurous, much younger Raleigh Gilbert took command. In the following spring a resupply ship arrived to find *'All things in good forwardness.'* The settlers had also constructed the first sailing ship to be built in North America naming her the 'Virginia' this being changed, much later, to the 'Virginia of Sagadahoc.'

In the autumn another ship arrived with the news that was to change the course of history. Raleigh Gilbert had inherited substantial estates in England on the death of his brother John. The colony's now wealthy leader opted to return home and pursue the life of an English gentleman. The remaining settlers chose to accompany him. They set sail, accompanying the supply ship in the 'Virginia', and returned to England. Fort St George was abandoned and the site fell into ruins. That would have been the end of the matter, except for an incredible piece of luck.

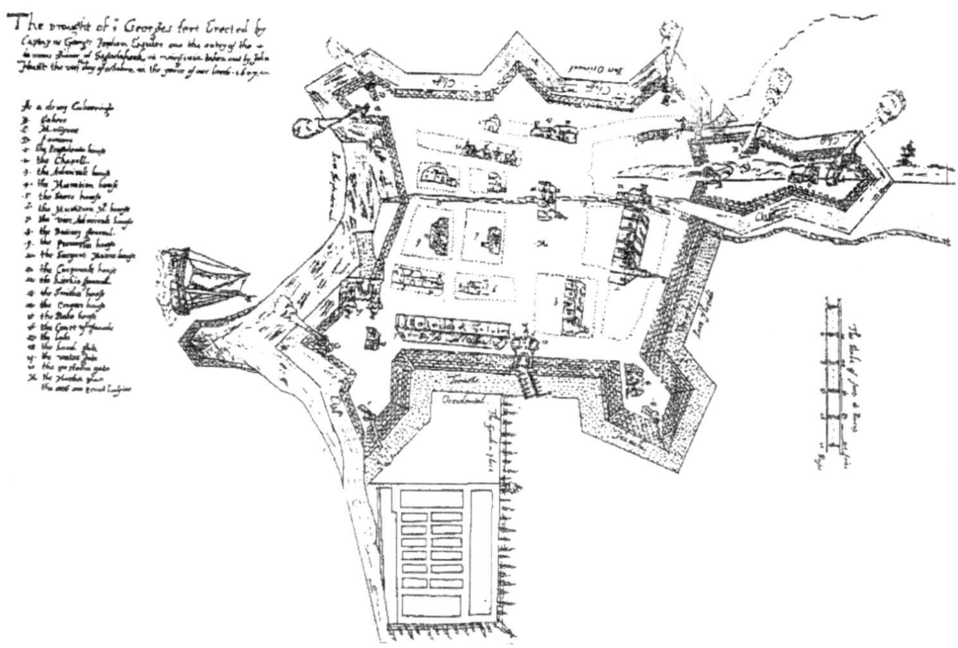

Map of the Popham Colony site drawn in 1607 by John Hunt

In 1607, some seven weeks after the settlers arrived, a map of the site was compiled by John Hunt, a military cartographer. When the settlers returned home they brought it with them and it somehow found its way into the hands of the Spanish ambassador to London. It was taken to Spain where it lay undiscovered in an archive until 1888. It is a unique record of a settlement of the period and the only known one in existence. As such it has been invaluable to archaeologists who started to excavate the site in 1994. Although it appears to record what was planned, rather than what was achieved, it has proved to be both detailed and accurate.

It helped them reveal what had lain hidden for nearly four centuries. The site provided a time capsule of life in 1607 - 8 which had been virtually undisturbed after its abandonment. This made it extremely important in developing an accurate picture of an early American settlement, as its contemporary Jamestown, had suffered constant disturbance. Excavations continue and to date a storehouse and Raleigh Gilbert's house have been uncovered. Over a thousand artefacts have been found including pottery, glass beads, a pipe bowl and stems, buttons, lead shot and bolts, armour and most important of all, a caulking iron used to seal joints in ships.

Memorial stone, at Popham Beach, Maine, to George Popham

The Darrell Legend

This legend is forever connected to the Popham family in that it is quoted as the reason why Sir John Popham acquired Littlecote. Its only link to Hunstrete is the curse applied to the Popham family, which I will enlarge upon later. However as it is the most well known story connected with the family, no book concerning them would be complete without it. It has been much embroidered down the years, was referred to by Aubrey the 17th century biographer and used as the subject of 'Rokeby' by Sir Walter Scott.

The Darrell family moved into Littlecote in 1415 when William Darrell of Yorkshire married Elizabeth De Calston and through her gained the family manor. In 1549 'Wild' William Darrell inherited the estate. His way of life caused much local consternation and gossip. The legend bearing his name is as follows

In the year 1575, apparently on a dark and stormy night, Darrell sent two of his servants to fetch Mother Barnes, a midwife living at Shefford in Berkshire. She was promised a rich reward if she would attend a lady who was about to give birth. On agreeing to do so she was blindfolded and taken on horseback, seated behind one of the messengers, to a house some distance away. She entered and was led upstairs to a large well furnished chamber, containing a blazing fire, where her blindfold was removed. From there she passed to a second chamber, richly hung with arras and thence to a third chamber, similarly luxurious. This contained a bed, upon which lay a gentlewoman, her face covered by a veil.

The midwife subsequently delivered a male child, early in the morning, and took it to the outer chamber to show the gentleman there. He bid her to cast it upon the fire. She begged and pleaded for the child's life, offering to raise it as her own. Her pleas went unheeded with the gentleman concerned either snatching the child from her and carrying out the deed himself, or forcing her to do his bidding. Afterwards the midwife was commanded to sit with the mother throughout the day. That same night she was returned to her village in the manner in which she had been fetched. The midwife being very disturbed by what had taken place is supposed to have surreptitiously cut off a small piece of the bed hangings and counted the stairs down from the chamber. Both of these were reportedly later used as evidence when the midwife, racked by guilt, made a deposition, or statement, as to what had happened.

Whether there is any truth in this story has been the subject of much speculation. Among Darrell's correspondence from Fleet prison in 1579 is a memorandum from Antonye Bridges. This was telling him that one of his neighbours, Lord Hertford, had been questioning Bridges as to whether Darrell knew of the deposition. When Bridges replied in the affirmative, the Earl demanded to know how William had reacted. Bridges finding him 'maliciously bent' against his

Littlecote House Hotel in Wiltshire (above), formerly the main seat of the Popham family, and (left) the tableau in the Darrell Chamber, in the hotel, which depicts the mysterious gentleman, the midwife and the newly delivered baby

adversary forwarded Darrell a copy of the deposition. This had been made before Bridges, by the midwife under oath, and referred to the story of a child murder (for full deposition see appendix 13).

A letter discovered at Longleat from Sir Henry Knyvett, of Charlton, to Sir John Thynne of Longleat appears to relate to the same incident. However Knyvett was another neighbour of Darrell and long time enemy. It was also rumoured that William was having an affair with his wife. The letter reads

> *"Sir,*
>
> *"I besetch you lett me crave so much favour of you as to procure your servant Mr. Bonham, moste effectually to examin his sister, tochinge her usage att Willm Dorrell's, the berth of her children, howe many they were, and what becam of them. She shall have no cawse off feare trulie, to confess the uttermost, for I will defend her from all perill howe so ever the case fall owte. The brute of the murder of one of them increaseth fowlely, and theare falleth owte such other heyghnous matter against him as will toche him to the quick.*
>
> *" From Charlton this ijth of January 1578.*
>
> *"Your loving friend,*
>
> *"H. KNYVETT*
>
> *"To the right worshipful and my very lovinge friend, Syr John Thynne, Kyght, Geve this."*

It is said that Darrell stood trial for the murder and that his judge was Sir John Popham. Legend has it that the plaintiff was acquitted in return for the gift of Littlecote. However there are several arguments against this:

Darrell was supposedly tried in 1582, but Popham didn't become a judge until 1595.

Sir John Popham was a distant relation of the childless Darrell and may have inherited Littlecote in return for his services. A likely scenario is that Sir John became a benefactor, in recognition of the benefits his legal advice had provided. This would have been given to Darrell in the many disputes with his neighbours, for which he was renown. Sir John may even have purchased Littlecote, as a bill of sale is said to exist among the Popham papers in the British Museum, although I have failed to trace this.

What transpired will probably remain the subject of debate, but by whatever means Sir John Popham had acquired a reversion on Littlecote by 1586 and the property became his when Darrell was killed by a fall from his horse in 1589.

With the estate came the curse attributed variously to the distraught mother of the dead child and to the midwife. This foretold that whatever family lived in the manor house would die out in the male line. Whether it is true or not is a matter for speculation. However Darrell died childless and the Popham estates have twice passed through the female line, with the last surviving members all being female. In 1804 General William Leyborne inherited through his mother, formerly Ann Popham, on condition that he assume the name and arms of the family. In 1804 this was done by Act of Parliament and the family became the Leyborne Pophams, their arms being quartered together.

They remained so until 1943 when Eric Tremayne Buller inherited through his mother, Elinor Louise Leyborne Popham, again as long as the family's name was adopted. He duly did this and became Buller Leyborne Popham. He had no male heirs so on his death the name died out apart from Ann Leyborne Popham, a spinster aunt who is 90 at the time of writing. With her demise will come the end of the Hunstrete branch, of a long and illustrious family lineage, bearing the name Popham.

Coincidentally and eerily, a large number of male heirs bearing the Popham name have died in infancy down through the generations.

Other Hunstrete Legends

I have repeatedly heard recounted and seen published, more than once, a wonderful story concerning the funeral of Dorothy Popham in 1797. It is said that she had requested to be buried at midnight, which apparently at one time was quite fashionable. Following her wishes her funeral cortege left Hunstrete at 11.00pm. Her coffin was carried on the shoulders of estate workers, the considerable distance to Marksbury church, followed by a procession of mourners, with the whole being lit by flaming torches.

It is also said that black gowns were provided and that after the funeral the mourners returned to Hunstrete House where cold meats, biscuits, beer and wine awaited them. The principal rooms and the staircase of the house were draped in black, a custom that by tradition continued for several months. Despite extensive searching I have yet to find the source of the above but like most legends there is probably some basis of truth in it, the story being passed down through oral tradition.

The same Dorothy Popham is said to have cast a handful of silver coins into the molten metal, when a tenor bell was being cast for Marksbury church, by the Bilbies of Chew Stoke. This was supposedly to sweeten the tone.

Another fascinating story concerns a moleskin coat, purported to have been made for one of the Popham ladies, from the skins of animals trapped on the estate. This would have been a fashionable item in the late Victorian and Edwardian eras, so it is probably true. As records show that hundreds were killed each year it would have been a talking point to have a garment made from one's own moles! The dead animal was skinned and the pelt pinned out on a board, often an old door, to dry in the sun. Each was then trimmed and the skins sewn together. A coat would have needed well over 200 skins.

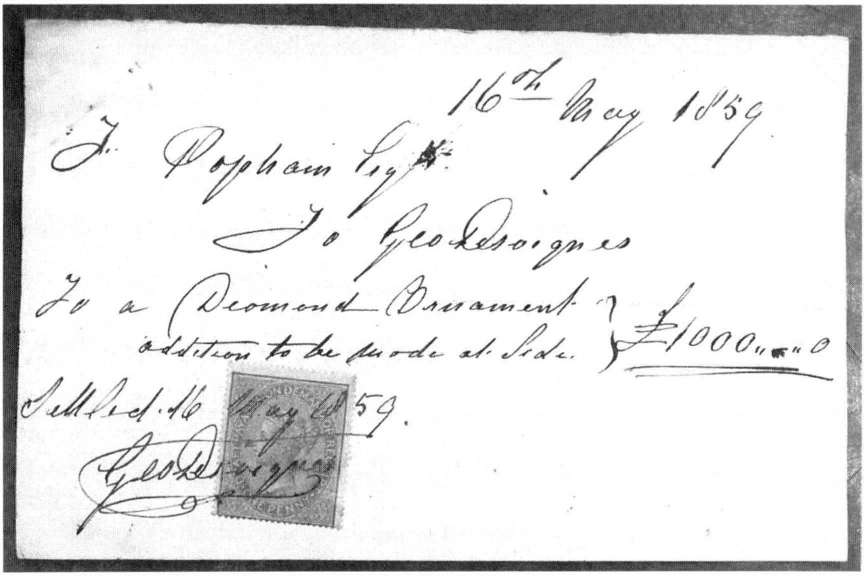
16th May 1859
J. Popham Esq.
To Geo Desoignes
To a Diamond Ornament addition to be made at Side } £1000..0
Settled 16 May 1859
Geo Desoignes

Receipt for item of jewellery

Over the course of the centuries the Popham family acquired a considerable collection of family jewels, an example being shown on the receipt illustrated. Legend has it that they once owned the finest collection of emeralds in the country but their whereabouts are no longer known. They may have been sold, with the rest of the pieces, to settle the debts incurred by Francis William Leyborne Popham (1862 - 1907), or may have been retained by his wife when they separated.

I have been told, by a member of the Popham family, that in the 19th century it was possible for the family to travel from Hunstrete to Littlecote without leaving their own land. Whether this was true or not, I do not know but they were certainly major landowners at this time.

Unlike Littlecote, which is reputedly haunted by the dead child, I know of no ghosts at Hunstrete. However various people have told me that the bedroom named Owl has a presence. Apparently they have felt cold when entering the room but no one has seen a ghost to date!

Bath Archaeological Trust has carried out two assessments at Hunstrete as prerequisites for planning permission being granted. These both took place in 1994. The first application in May of that year concerned the site of the mediaeval mansion complex. It was made by Bathampton Angling Association and was in relation to the development of the Hunstrete fishing complex. As this involved fairly major disturbance an excavation was carried out.

Excavation trench near Hunstrete lake

Mediaeval stonework uncovered during excavations, probably part of a causeway

The aim was to establish what archaeological features and deposits survived on site, what their level of preservation was and what they represented. From this they would decide what recommendations to make. A representative sample of six trenches was excavated across the site, initially by mechanical diggers, to remove the topsoil and also a large quantity of red marl found in several of them. This appears to have come from the bank about 100 yards to the south, which was cut away to form a plateau on which to build the Grand Mansion. The remainder was then excavated by hand. For the location of these see the accompanying map.

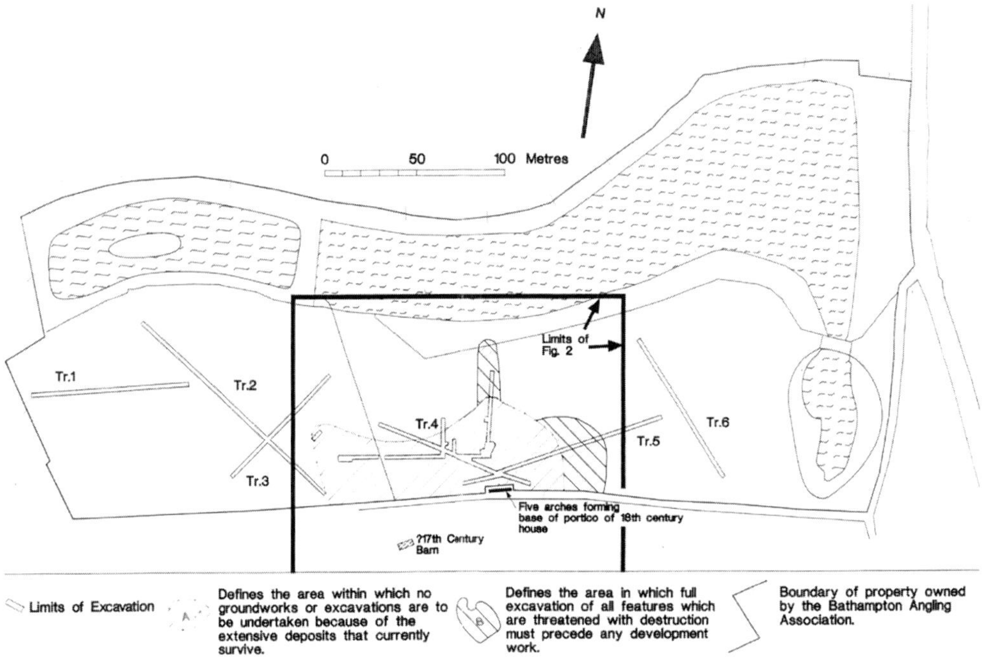

Position of excavation trenches at Hunstrete lake

As expected, most archaeological evidence was found in Trench 4, this being nearest to the site of the mediaeval manor. It contained:

A substantial revetment wall set inside the face of a shallow moat

A break in this wall containing steps flanked by splayed stone and brick walls

A cobbled surface leading from the base of the steps

What appears to be a garden path running due north from the cobbled area towards the lake.

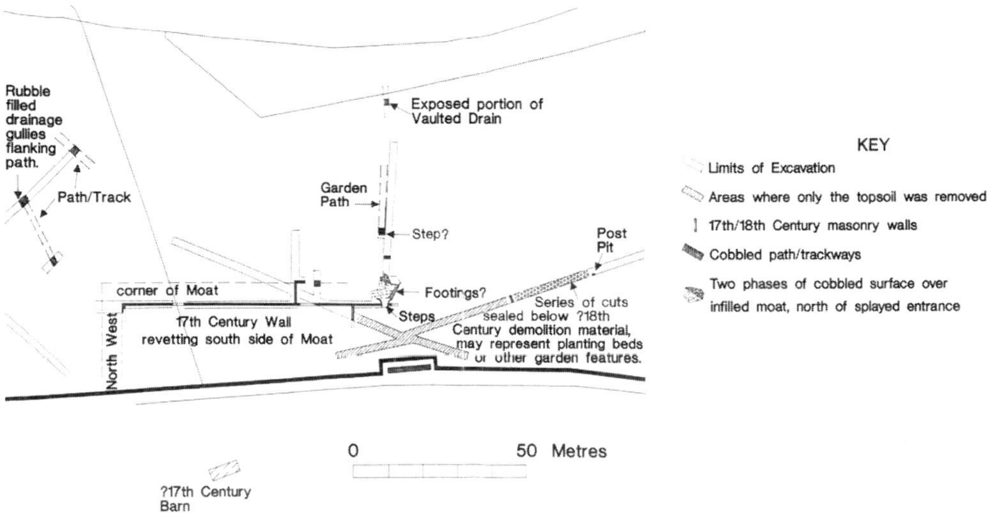

Detail of excavation trench 4

The moat had been backfilled and a short two metre wide section was excavated through the infill. A dark charcoaly grey silt in the base contained several clay pipe bowls dated between 1640 - 1660. These bear the name Jeffry Hunt, a member of a famous pipe making family, from Norton St. Philip, near Bath.

This suggested that the life span had been relatively short. As the moat was known to be earlier than this, a second one may lie further south or the original may have been reworked. Further excavation revealed the north west corner of the moat, walls, a large stone packed posthole, presumably for a door post and a crude cobbled track or yard surface, distinctly worn in places. The top of a stone built vaulted drain that was uncovered is thought to be a conduit to take excess water from the moat.

A pale grey stone slab some 1.75m long, 55cm wide and 20 cm thick was also found and parts of a path to the north extending for about seven metres. The slab is thought to be part of terracing, used in the construction of formal gardens, in order to accommodate the slope of the land and the path a garden walkway. This would be in keeping with the documentary evidence that refers to gardens in 1252, 1305 and 1517.

Trench 1 contained no archaeological features, whilst trench 2 only contained field drains. Trench 3 also had field drains and the remains of a large tree root ball that may have been one of those shown on the 1759 map (see page 6), as an easterly avenue of trees bisecting the lake, as its relative position corresponds well. Both trenches 2 and 3 contained large quantities of red marl, and their

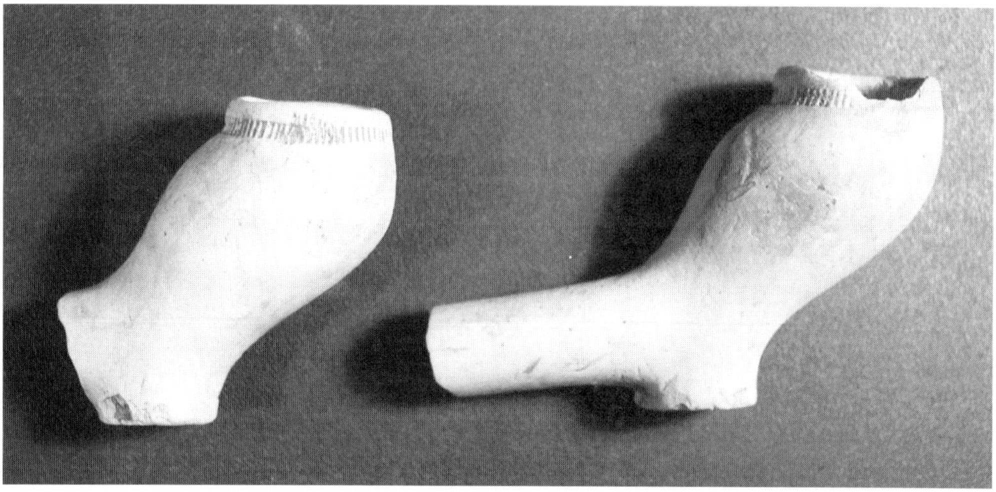

Clay pipe bowls c. 1640-1660 from the moat at Hunstrete

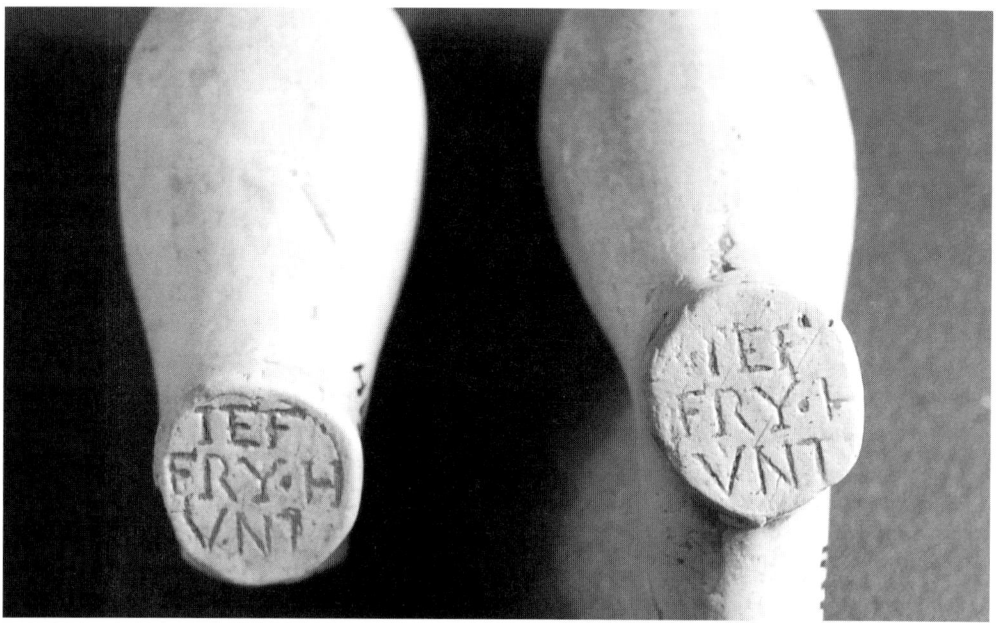

Detail of the base of the pipe bowls showing the maker's mark

position, in a damp and boggy depression, would make them the ideal place to dispose of soil when the terrace for the Grand Mansion was constructed. The evidence suggests that the topsoil was first removed and replaced after the deposition of the red marl. This would be in keeping with the landscaping of the house.

Slab thought to be part of the terracing for the formal mediaeval gardens

Trench 5 contained a massive quantity of rubble that represented the wholesale demolition of a large structure or series of structures. This would have been the buildings demolished to facilitate the construction of the Grand Mansion. None of the finds within the rubble were earlier than mid 18th century. It also contained a wall from which the stone had been extensively robbed. Like trenches 2 and 3 the topsoil had been removed and later replaced.

A number of broad shallow cuts were also found, filled with a variety of materials, and may have been garden features. Part of the drive to the Grand Mansion was uncovered, being composed of a compact spread of hard and partially crushed, small red marl nodules. The deposits were quite extensive and coincided well with the anticipated position of the oval terminus on the 1759 map (see page 6). Further evidence of this was also found in Trench 4. There were also portions of several land drains in Trench 5.

Trench 6 contained no archaeological features apart from land drains. It did however have deposits similar to Trench 5, these being spreads of red marl sealing underlying demolition material.

The survey recommended that the area A shown on the trench plan (see page 164) warranted preservation in situ and no disturbance should be permitted. The area marked B merited full archaeological excavation and recording of the features before any earth moving activity was allowed.

All the finds from the site have been deposited with the Bath Museums Service at the Roman Baths Museum and may be viewed by appointment.

The second application was in December 1994 and concerned the area of the car park. It was made by Arcadian U.K. Developments Limited, who purchased the hotel in 1991 and wished to build a leisure centre on site, some hundred metres north west of the main complex. Part of the land formed the car park whilst the remainder was unused. To the west lay part of the formal gardens and the map of 1759 indicated that further elements, that had remained relatively undisturbed, were beneath this area. The initial archaeological survey concluded that this presented an opportunity to investigate the layout and features of the formal garden and establish the likely date of its construction.

The Bath Archaeological Trust recommended a programme of limited excavation, the results of which would determine whether any further work was necessary. In the event the proposed development did not take place with Arcadian selling the hotel in 1996.

In 2002 two amateur archaeologists, Lynne Langan and Chris Saunders were given permission to carry out a survey of Hunstrete. Detailed planning then took place including the use of documentary evidence, a range of maps, aerial photographs, and initial field walking to gain a better understanding of the site. Consent was obtained from the relevant authorities before a systematic search, of the most likely locations to yield artefacts, within the estate grounds was begun, using a sophisticated metal detector.

Each find was mapped with a global positioning satellite to record its exact location, its depth recorded, photographed, catalogued and where possible identified. The task is monumental and a complete survey will take years. However Hunstrete immediately began to yield up its treasures.

To date finds have included items such as:

Pottery from a number of periods

Coins including Roman examples and a George III cartwheel penny so nicknamed due to its large size and weight

Buckles, including an early mediaeval one, from a shoe which shows traces of gilt and a Tudor example, named after its spectacle shape

A book clasp from the mediaeval period

A pendant thought to be mediaeval

An 18th century sword pommel

A rein guide of the same date

A 19th brass saddle plate embossed with the initials FWLP

Several brass labels from varieties of rose bushes, apples and pears of the late 19th, early 20th century

Silver items including a broken candlestick and several thimbles

The most exciting find of all, to date, has been of a number of musket balls from the Civil War period, together with two cannon balls. The location, in which most of these were found, was exactly where one would have expected the soldiers to be camped, given the topography of the estate. It certainly gives added credence to the accounts of the troops being billeted here prior to the siege of Wells. It also underlines what can be achieved when metal detecting is carried out in combination with documentary evidence.

The finds will be cleaned, conserved, where applicable, and will ultimately form part of a permanent display in the hotel.

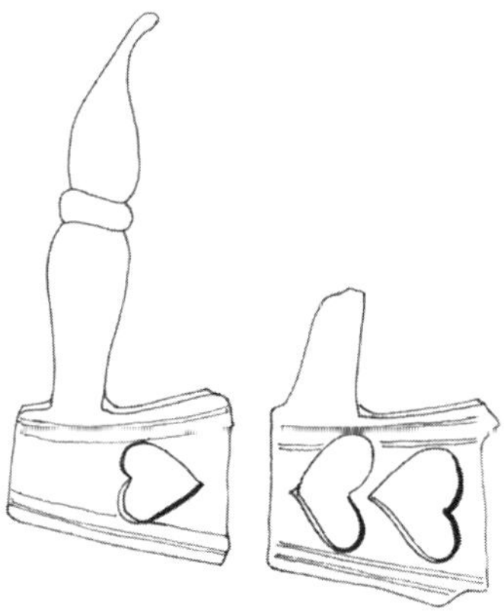

Unidentified item made of Bronze

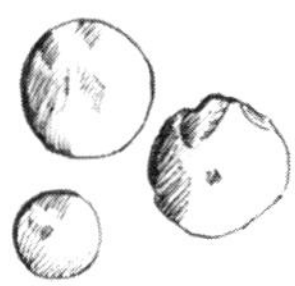

Musket Balls

Brass Saddle Plate

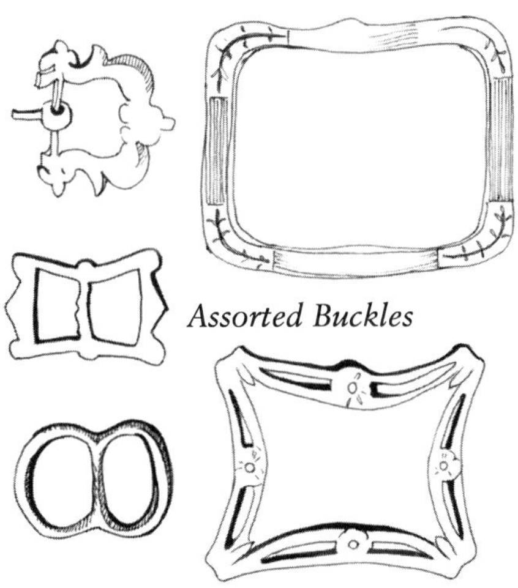

Assorted Buckles

Book Clasp

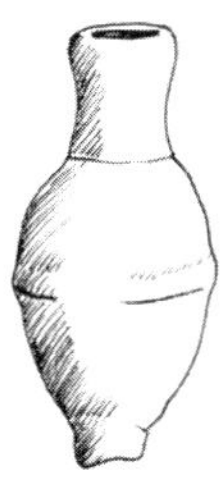

Sword Pommel

The Popham family had a marked effect on the development of a much wider area of north east Somerset than Hunstrete. They ultimately owned a number of local manors including: Compton Dando, Chelwood, Marksbury, Publow, Woollard, Pensford, Timsbury, Farmborough, Queen Charlton, Dundry, Chew Magna and Brislington. Slightly farther afield they had a Decoy Pond at Nyland which would have been for the trapping of wild ducks that wintered on the Somerset Levels. Their influence can still be seen in many of these villages.

A Popham window with its characteristic small panes

Many of the houses were built to a similar design and can be identified by both the style and the characteristic Popham small paned metal casement windows with their ornate catches. Several examples can be seen in Woollard close to the bridge and in the Carpenter's Arms at Stanton Wick. Whether the latter was ever owned by the Pophams, or whether the windows were reused from a former estate property, I have yet to establish.

Others still bear the Popham estate numbering with Compton Dando having 206 and 207 in Cocker's Hill and 208 - 211 in Court Hill. Many cottages still display evidence of Popham ownership in their interior with the initials FWLP and EWLP carved into woodwork including door frames and panels, stair treads and risers and roof timbers. Others have the same initials carved into stonework particularly within the supporting structure. Keeper's cottage in Hunstrete has an ornate plaque above the front door depicting the letter P, a form of identification not seen elsewhere, although the manor house at Farmborough has the date 1667 and the initials AP above the main entrance.

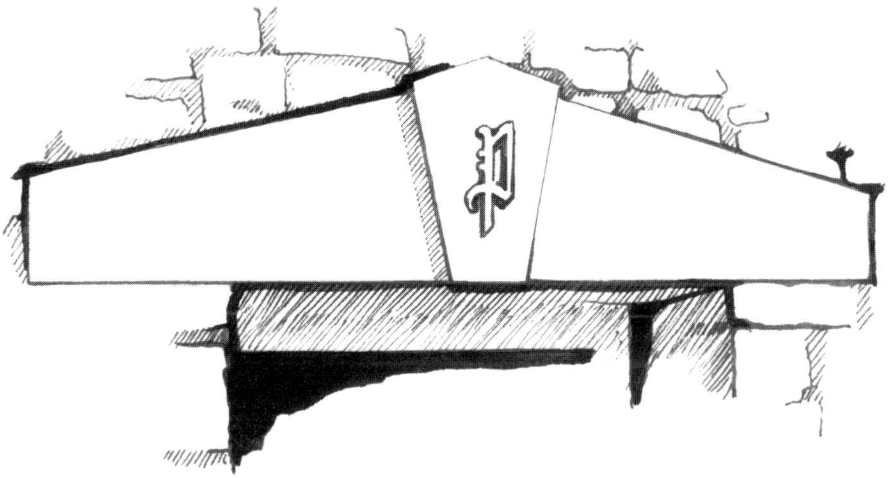

The plaque above the door of number 9 Hunstrete

The church at Marksbury contains several memorials to the Popham family together with entries in the parish registers and headstones in the churchyard. There are two tablets on the interior walls of the church with the following inscriptions

> *To the Memory of*
> *FRANCIS POPHAM Esq.*
> *Elder son of EDWARD POPHAM*
> *One of the Representatives in Several*
> *Parliaments for the County of Wilts.*
> *Descended from*
> *Lord Chief Justice POPHAM*
> *And Heir to the Fortunes*
> *As well as the Virtues of the family*
> *Distinguished by its attachment*
> *To the Interest of their Country*
> *This Monument is Erected by his Widow*
> *in Testimony of her Affection*
> *Ob. 14. Feb 1779 AE 45*

Also
Of DOROTHY his Wife
Eldest Daughter and Coheiress
of D: Matthew HUTTON
Archbishop of Canterbury
the Younger Brother
of JOHN HUTTON Esq.
of Marske in the County of York
OB. 14 July 1797 AE 64

IN LOVING MEMORY OF
FRANCIS WILLIAM LEYBORNE POPHAM
OF LITTLECOTE SON OF
FRANCIS LEYBORNE POPHAM
BORN 8 MARCH 1862 DIED 15 JULY 1907

A brass plaque records the gift of lighting

Light installed in church was the gift of
Hugh FA Leyborne Popham and his wife Janet to
Commemorate Coronation of King George VI and Queen Elizabeth
12. May. 1937
The congregation gave this tablet

A further plaque records the gift of electricity to the church by the Buller Leybourne Pophams.

Several gravestones in Marksbury churchyard mark the remains of members of the Popham family, these being:

Major E.T.Buller Leyborne Popham M.C.
Duke of Cornwall Light Infantry
3rd January 1894
8th August 1973
Farewell
Also his wife
Dorothy Bridget
14th March 1894
9th July 1998

Elizabeth Gwendoline Buller
7th September 1902 - 2nd July 1945
And
Millicent Gwendoline Buller

However most of the family's christenings, marriages and burials took place at Chilton Foliat in Wiltshire, this being the parish of their main seat at Littlecote.

In the church there are various memorial tablets on the walls:

Dorothy Leyborne Popham July 7th 1830 aged 18
Elizabeth Leyborne Popham Dec. 28th 1832 aged 19
Daughters of lieut. General Popham and Elizabeth

FWLP March 8th 1862 - July 15th 1907

William Leyborne third son of the late William Leyborne Leyborne of Westwell and Ann his wife, daughter of the late Edward Popham of Littlecote. Died Dec.28th 1790 aged 17

Edward Popham (rector) youngest son of Edward Popham of Littlecote. Sept. 16th 1815

Ann widow of William Leyborne Leyborne (died 1775) and mother of General Popham of Littlecote - only surviving son

General EWLP of Littlecote died June 16th 1843 aged 79 and Elizabeth his wife died March 1st 1836 aged 52

Francis Hugh Leyborne Popham
Jan 19th 1861 to June 21st 1861

Francis Leyborne Popham 2nd son of General Edward Leyborne Popham 14th October 1809 - 30th July 1880

Elizabeth Leyborne Popham his wife 26th July 1833 - 21st August 1865

And also their son Hugh Francis Arthur 1864 - 1943 and his wife Janet Emily 1884 - 1946

Francis wife of Revd. J.L. Popham August 16th 1839 aged 27

There is also a plaque recording the rectors of Chilton Foliat among them:

1714 - 1743 George Popham MA
1779 - 1816 Edward Popham DD
1835 - 1873 Canon John Leyborne Popham

The exception to this is Sir John Popham and his family, who occupy a magnificent tomb in the parish church at Wellington in Somerset, their home for some years. Also at Wellington is an almshouse endowed by him, initially erected in 1606, for six poor and aged men, and the same number of women in similar circumstances.

Thefamily tomb at Wellington church
showing the seven daughters and five sons of Sir Francis Popham

It was rebuilt in 1833 and in the early part of the 20th century converted to flats for elderly people.

Besides the visible evidence of their influence on the area, there exists a wealth of memories and anecdotal tales of the Popham family, many of which have been passed down through the generations. In the fullness of time some have become legend. Mention the name Popham, particularly amongst the older generation and the tales will start to flow. Fading memories, poetic licence and half remembered truths have all played their part but in essence the Popham story lives on.

The Popham Papers

The Popham Papers is the collective name given to the mass of documentary evidence left by the Popham Family concerning their estates. Those related to their holdings in Somerset are stored in the County Record Office in Taunton under the accession numbers DD PO and DD Pot. There is such a wealth of information that the catalogue for the former runs to 100 pages and the latter 50 pages. They comprise court rolls, leases, rentals, account books, payment vouchers, maps and schedules, surveys, inventories, correspondence and sale catalogues. This is in addition to any material available from other sources such as the Parish Records for Marksbury, Census Returns, the Tithe Map and Schedule for Marksbury and so on.

The sheer volume of material makes the task of researching the Hunstrete Estate an extremely daunting one. For example DD PO 32 comprises 112 bundles of documents dating from 1649 to 1817. Each contains up to a further dozen bundles, made up of about 100 small strips of paper folded in half. Untying, unfolding and deciphering these is a time consuming and often frustrating task, as many are illegible, with the vast majority adding little to the Hunstrete story.

Similarly many of the other documents are in Latin, particularly the early ones, and others indecipherable. Some are too damaged to be used, whilst others are obviously missing. This is particularly so in relation to the houses in Hunstrete and the surrounding area. Local rumour has it that those records concerned with building were stored in a room at the estate yard. In the 1950's, during a clear out, it appears that these were inadvertently burned by an over enthusiastic youngster. Whether this is true is a matter for speculation, but there does seem to be a marked absence of records concerning building work, apart from the Grand Mansion, together with accounts for maintenance and repair.

The earliest records date from the 17th century although these tend to be somewhat sparse, with the most comprehensive ones being from the early part of the 19th century.

Tapestries

Many of the Popham ladies were keen needlewomen and there are tapestries in Wells Cathedral worked by members of the last three generations. Beatrice Salter, embroidered some of the kneelers, her mother, Mary Corbin, a bench seat cover in grey with gold crosses and her grandmother, Janet Leyborne Popham, two hangings in the choir stalls, which bear her name.

Beatrice's mother also copied the design of the bed hangings in the Darrell chamber at Littlecote and made the tapestry into curtains for her bedroom at Hunstrete Cottage.

The New World Tapestry was conceived by Tom More, as a representation of the exploration of the New World from 1583 to 1642. It is the world's biggest stitched embroidery being 267 feet by four feet and comprises 24 panels each 11 feet long. It was started in 1976 and was stitched by 20 teams of tapissiers, made up of 256 volunteers. The Queen, Prince Philip, the Queen Mother, the Princess Royal and the Duchess of Gloucester have all made Royal stitches in gold wool. Prince Charles added the last stitch in 2000.

The panels contain 264 armorial shields, the Pophams among them. These alternate along the length of its top and bottom borders with illustrations of the same number of the flowers of herbs, medicinal plants, trees and shrubs. These are included because the colonists took ointments and cures with them on their voyages and the New World explorers brought such plants as the potato and tobacco.

It features the Popham family on several of the panels, these being 1605, 1606 and 1607 - 1608. It is housed in the British and Commonwealth Museum at Bristol.

Portraits

There are numerous portraits of the Popham family located in a variety of places. The most accessible of these are at Littlecote House Hotel and at the Bristol Museum and Art Gallery. The portraits at the former include those of Sir John Popham and Colonel Alexander Popham. At the latter are two portraits by Gainsborough that have been the subject of much debate. They are now generally agreed to be marriage portraits of William Leyborne Leyborne and Ann Leyborne, formerly Popham.

Ann Leyborne (nee Popham) and William Leyborne Leyborne

There are several other portraits held by members of the family, together with a marble bust of Francis Popham and a painting of the 1855 Derby winner ' Wild Darrell'. This horse was owned by Francis Leyborne Popham and was bred and trained at Littlecote.

Appendix 1

The Anglo Saxon Charter

This is a translation of the original Anglo Saxon charter recording the boundaries of land at Marksbury (Merkesburi) and Hunstrete (Houndstreet) given by King Athelstan to the Nobleman Ethelelm in AD936. It is thought to be a 12th century copy of the original.

To Red Ford
This is on the boundary between Marksbury and Priston and is a crossing of the Conygre brook.

Then along the Brook to the north east side of the warren (Conigrave)
This is along the Conygre brook which runs from Priston to Farmborough. As rabbits were not introduced into Britain until the Norman invasion, this suggests that this is a copy.

Then straight on to the south side of Wether Grove
This is south of Marksbury village where there is a field called Willgrove.

Then by the foot of the slope to the gate by the Alder trees
This is presumably the slope near the location of the New Inn at Farmborough.

Then by the south side of Middle Grove
This is along the line of the road from the New Inn at Farmborough westwards.

Then along the track
This track still runs west above Whidcombe Brake.

And the track bears west

Then to the south of the Wide Combe
This is still the boundary between Farmborough and Chelwood and the Wide Combe (Whidcombe) is very obvious. The fields still bear the name Widcombe.

Along Wide Combe to South Brook
This is the turning north along the Chelwood parish boundary.

Along the Brook to the Hollow Dyke
This is the deep ravine in the wood to the west of Hunstrete House.

Then along the Boundary Game Enclosure to Bald Down
This circles around the present parkland of Hunstrete House and probably follows the line of Compton Dando parish boundary through the field to the north of the Hawhaw. This was Bald Down.

Then along Bald Down to the east end of the Ploughland
The charter boundary now turns east through the land of Wick Farm towards Common Wood.

Then north to a grove
This was presumably Atgrove Wood.

Then to the foot of a slope
Probably the slope running down to Tucking Mill.

Then along a narrow way
The small by-road east of Tucking Mill.

Then to Woden's Dyke and four acres north of the dyke
This refers to the Wansdyke and the two smaller fields which still exist on either side by the junction of the B3116 with the A39.

From Woden's Dyke (Wansdyke) to Wirtalen
Wirtalen is the hill south of Stantonbury that is now called Winsbury.

Then to Winck's Camp
This is the fortification that can still be seen on the top of Winsbury Hill.

Then along the Ploughland
The route must turn south somewhere on the level ground between Marksbury and Stanton Prior.

Then along the Stone Way to the Red Ford
This must be the road between Marksbury and Priston thus completing the circuit.

Reproduced with special thanks to Dr Joe Bettey who recreated instructions for the contemporary route.

Appendix 2

The Domesday Entry For Marksbury

> *The church itself holds Mercesberie. In the time of King Edward it gelded for 10 hides. The arable is 8 carucates. Thereof in demense are 4 hides and a half, and there are 2 carucates, and 5 servants, and 6 villanes, and 5 cottagers, with 3 ploughs. There are 19 acres of meadow, and 40 acres of wood. It is worth £10.*
>
> *Of the land a Thane holds 2 hides and a half. It is worth 20s. Oswald held it in the time of King Edward, and it could not be separated from the church.*

A hide was a measurement of land of approximately 160 acres.

A carucate was a unit of taxation. Originally it was the amount of land that a team of oxen could plough in a year. It varied according to the type of soil but was approximately 120 acres.

The demesne was the land on a manor reserved for the Lord's own use, as distinct from land held by tenants.

Villanes were tenants tied to the land and required to work on the demesne.

Cottagers held cottages, sometimes with a smallholding. They were obliged to work on the Lord's land, either for free or for a fixed sum.

A thane was an Anglo Saxon landowner, who held his land by charter, in return for military service.

Appendix 3

Inventory of 1646

A true and
perfect inventorye of all and singular the goodes, Chattells and debtes of Sir Francis Popham Knight late of Hunstreete in the Countie of Somersett, deceased, viewed and appraised the first, sixth and twenty fourth dayes of March Anno Do'mi 1646 by John Locke of Pensford and James Burges of Stanton Drew in the said Countye as followeth vizt.

Inprimis all the Plate	£70
Att Hunstreete in the greate dineing Roome foure peaces of arras, hangings, twae table boardes, two side boardes, one Couche, twentie Chaires, the stooles, Carpettes, Cushions and other necessaries in that Roome	£30
Item in the best Chamber one standing bedstedd, a featherbed with ites furniture, curtaines, Vallence hangings and other necessaryes in that Chamber	£20
Item in the Kitchen Chamber one standing bedstedd, one trundle bedstedd, three featherbeddes, Curtaines, Vallence, hangings, a sideboarde and other furniture	£10
Item in the next lodgings one standing beddstedd, one	

halfe head bedstedd, foure feathbedes, Curtaines, Vallens, one red silke quilt, Ruggs, Coverlettes blanckettes, foure Chaires, five stooles, one table board, and other small utensills	£10
Item in the Ladyes Chamber twoe bedsteddes, twoe feather -beddes with blacke hangings and other furniture to those beddes, one Chest, one side Cupboard, twoe trunkes, twoe Chaires, three stooles and other necessaryes	£10
Item in the yellow Chamber one side table, one standing bedstedd, and featherbedd, Curtaines, Vallens and other furniture	£3
Item in the Nursery Chamber one standing bedstedd, one featherbedd, Curtaines, Vallence, hangings, a Couch, the Chaires, stooles and other utensills	£10
Item in the Gallery, three bedsteddes, three bedes, & their furniture, the Chestes, trunckes, hutches, and many other implements	£5
Items in the Chamber by the Gallery, one bedstedd with Curtaines, one featherbedd with ites furniture, one Chaire & other small things	40s

Item in the Captaines Chamber,
& the little Chamber adjoyneing,
three bedsteddes, two featherbeddes,
one flockebed with their
furniture, Curtaines, hangings,
three Chaires, and other
necessaryes £8

(Kitchen)
spittes
great iron (here the parchment is torn)
fryeing pans,
pans, twoe brasse ladles,
two brasse skimers, the
potthookes, hangers, Cleavers,
chopping knyves, and
other necessaryes for the
kitchen

Item in the Larder and
the Pastry, the Table -
boardes, tubbs, and other
necessaryes 40s

Item in the Wash - house,
one furnace and one
brasse pan 50s

Item in the Brew - house
one washing vate, one
Cooler, one Keeve, other
tymber vessells for that
use and all the hogsheades
and barrells £6 14s 4d

Item in the Hall, three
table boardes, three formes,
one Iron grate in the
Chimney and one &
twenty muskettes £12

Item a Bell to ring to
Prayers and a Clocke
with a Bell £5

Item in the Closett diverse small thinges	£3 10s
Item all the bookes	£6 13s 4d
Item all the Lynnen	£100 *
Item all the pewter	£30
Item in the Porters Lodge in the foure Chambers there, one featherbedd & seaven other beddes, with the bedsteddes and their furniture, twoe Chaires, one peece of new sack - Cloth for a wynnoweing sheete and other small things	£5 10s
Item two horse beastes for the Coach, the markett mare and two Colehorses	£27
Item one New hackneye Saddle, and other saddles and horse furniture	£5
Item the Coach with ites furniture	£3 10s
Item sixe swine	£3 6s 8d

*this is the figure in the original manuscript, but it could be an error.

A copy of part of an inventory made two years after the death of Sir Francis Popham (1573 - 1644). Originally written on narrow lengths of parchment each about two feet long, stitched together, end to end, to form a long roll. The latter part of the inventory is missing. The document was discovered in a chest at Littlecote House, Wiltshire, and is now in private hands.

Appendix 4

Will of Dorothy Popham - 27th April 1797

DOROTHY POPHAM of Littlecote in the County of Wilts Widow and Relict of Francis Popham late of the same place Esqre being seised in fee under the Will of her sd husband by her Will of this date duly executed and attested gave and devised

ALL her estates at Houndstreet and Littlecott

UNTO Francis Popham of Houndstreet afsd. Esqre and his afsd for his life only he or they committing or suffering no manner of waste spoil or destruction in or to upon about the sd real estates or any of them or any part thereof at ant time or times during his natural life but always preserving and keeping the same and all and every the capital and other messuages and tenements edifices erections and buildings thereon and thereto belonging in a good sufficient and proper repair order and conditions for and during the trem of his natural life save and except that sd Francis Popham should have full power to cut timber to keep the same buildings in proper repair with Remr

To trustees upon trust to support contingent remainders etc Remr

Unto the first and every other son of sd Francis Popham in tail male Remr

Unto Lieut Col Edward William Leyborne and his ass's for life he or they committing or suffering no waste nor cutting down any timber other than and excapt for the purposes herein before mentioned Remr

Unto the first son and every other the son and sons of the body of sd Edward William Leyborne lawfully begotten or to be begotten severally and successively in remainder in tail male with divers remainders over

AND said Testatrix did order and direct that the person or persons becoming entitled to the possession of and should be resident in either of her Mansion Houses in Littlecott or Houndstreet should have free liberty to take away and use all or any part of her plate given by her as her heir looms from the Mansion House in which he or they might not happen to reside.

Appendix 5

Survey of 1831

Many of the principal beams lentils and joists very decayed and the parts that bear in the walls quite rotted off and that in consequence thereof the ceilings are falling down in various parts of the building That the plaistering and ornamental work also the works of the different trades are in a ruinous state (that is to say) the masons carpenters plaisterers and painters work and that every branch of such work is getting worse every day also that the ground floors are in a very bad state the joists quite rotted and the floors sinking and giving way that the beams are insecure and in a very dangerous state and cannot long support the pressure upon them And this dept also said that according to the best of his judgement I belief the expense of pulling down the said Mansion and sorting out the different materials and putting them in saleable lots will amount to about £600 And this Deponent also said that the dry rot is got into many parts of the principal timbers of the said Mansion and must in a very short time be attended with very serious consequences unless a thorough repair be immediately made to the building and that much of the timber will be of little value if left to remain longer in its present state And this deponent further saith that from the general decay of the said Mansion the cost of putting the same even into a secure state would according to the best of his judgement and belief amount to the sum of £5 000 at the least but that if the said Mansion was to be put into perfect repair and all the ornamental work restored to its original state it would cost the sum of £15 000 at the least And further than this Affidavit .... states supposing the building to be taken down that the materials would sell for £6 800 and to put those materials in a proper state to bring them to sale would cost £500. Considering the unfinished state of the Mansion at Mrs Pophams decease and that to perfect the original design would cost at least £60 000 and also taking into consideration the large sum required to put it even into a secure state as well as the enormous sum of £15 000 to put it into its original state which Genl. Popham as Tenant for Life does not feel himself justified in expending and if expended it is not very probable that the Mansion would ever be occupied and as the estate attached to Houndstreet comprises many Farms upon which New Farm Houses are absolutely wanted he feels anxious to rid the estate of a nuisance by pulling down the Mansion and applying the whole of the money arising from the Sale of the materials in building New Farm Houses which would add considerably to the improvement and value of the estate.

Appendix 6

Prior Park Sale Catalogue

The Prior Park sale was conducted by Messrs. English and Son on Tuesday 15th June 1847 and the following day. The cover of the catalogue offered for sale:

> A vast quantity of Material and Ornamental
> DECORATIONS AND DRESSINGS
> of
> HOUNDSTREET HOUSE
> Purchased by the late RIGHT REV. DR. BAINES
> In 1834 for the purpose of removing and applying
> its costly and valuable external and internal
> Decorations to the Restoration of PRIOR PARK
> And where a large portion has been used, and now forms
> the principal features of decoration at that superb Mansion

The 1834 date of purchase, of the dismantled Hunstrete House, shown on the above is an error and should read 1836. Prior Park was not destroyed by fire until this date and the above specifically mentions the restoration.

The items listed that came from the Grand Mansion were:

Oak, Ash, Oriental Plane and other Plank

LOT 1 A lot of wood, various
2 A lot of oak and cedar
3 Two pieces of ash and lot of sundries
4 Three plaster door cornices, 4 semicircular niches, a ceiling ornament and 2 semicircular pieces
5 Sundry pieces of oak and yew and a lot of centerings
6 Seven planks of oriental plane wood
7 Seven planks of beech and 12 of oak
8 Twenty - four planks of oak
9 Quantity of oak quarter
10 Twenty - four planks of oak
11 Nineteen ditto ditto
12 Twenty - four ditto ditto
13 Sundry pieces of oak and ash
14 Five planks of cedar

Sculpture in Stone, Balustrades, Etc, Etc. highly wrought

LOT 15 Forty iron balustrades
16 Forty ditto
17 Forty ditto
18 Forty ditto, more or less
19 Forty ditto more or less
20 One hundred and four feet of iron moulded handrail
21 Quantity of marble
22 Six wheel - stocks and 16 pieces of oak, ash and apple tree
23 Thirteen pieces of oak, various
24 Two circular sunflower ornaments, sculpted in freestone
25 Two ovals - Sacrificing a Ram, and Vulcan forging Arms - bodily sculpted in alto relievo
26 A square ditto - Astrobal brought prisoner before Scipio
27 A ditto - A Mythical subject
28 A ditto - A Group of Warriors
29 A ditto - A Mythical subject
30 Two - A Sunflower and Hercules resting from his labours
31 The moulded stone - work of 2 arches and five mask - head sculptured key stones

Oriental Plane Plank Etc. (continued)

LOT 32 Nine planks of oriental plane wood of extraordinary fine figure
33 Seven ditto
34 Twenty - four ditto
35 Twenty - four ditto
36 Twenty - four ditto
37 Thirty - six ditto
38 Seven planks of ditto
39 Quantity of oak, ash, acacia, thorn and maple
40 Thirty - three pieces of yew
41 Twenty - four pieces of oriental plane, same as above
42 Six planks of ditto
43 Six ditto
44 Seven ditto
45 Handsome stone balustrade for a terrace, 46 feet long, with carved therm - shaped balustrades, seven massive pedestals, with egg and tongue, and leaf mouldings
46 Handsome sculpted stone frieze, scroll pattern, 42 feet long
47 Moulded stone sill course, with egg and tongue, and leaf mouldings, 27 ft., and architrave head.

Rare Marbles

LOT 48 Five pieces of marble and sundry small pieces
49 Sienna marble slab, 5 ft. 10 by 3 ft. and another 4 ft. 10 by 2 ft. 5
50 Handsome Italian inlaid table top, 2 ft. 11 square, composed of jasper, brocatelli, sienna and other marbles
51 Veined marble slab, 7 ft. 3 long, 3 ft. wide
52 Very beautiful flower jasper slab, 4 ft. 2 long by 2 ft. wide
53 Verde antique marble slab, 3 ft. 11 long, by 2 ft. wide
54 Ditto, same size, and to match
55 Veined marble slab, 7ft. by 4ft.
56 Ditto ditto 5 ft. by 2ft.
57 Ditto ditto 5ft. 2 by 2ft. 4
58 Five pieces of marble and part of a chimney - piece
59 Dove marble chimney - piece, 3ft.
60 1 in. opening and hearth slab
61 Part of two chimney - pieces and hearth slab
62 Pair of half - circular marble slabs and veined marble slab
63 Pair of very beautiful sienna marble console slabs, 3 ft. 9 by 2 ft.
64 Pair of sienna marble ditto, 3 ft. 7 by 1 ft. 10
65 A lot
66 A lot

Original Carved Models, designed for Houndstreet House, cut for Plaster Castings, Trusses, Etc. Etc.

LOT 67 Twenty models carved in wood for casting plaster ornaments
68 Twenty ditto
69 Twenty ditto
70 A lot of ditto
71 A lot of ditto
72 Twenty ditto
73 Ten ditto
74 Six pair of richly - carved trusses and 4 pieces of moulding
75 Twenty Carton pierre Ionic pilaster caps and sundry plaster casts
76 Eighteen ditto and sundry plaster casts
77 Fifty - two Carton pierre wreaths, 13 plaster trusses and sundry casts
78 A lot of casts, various
79 A lot
80 Carpenter's bench
81 Ditto
82 Mahogany table and sundry furniture
83 Bookcase

84 HANDSOME OAK PULPIT, with reading - desk, steps, panelled sounding-board and fluted Ionic column
85 A lot

Glazed Sashes

LOT 86 Four pairs of oak glazed sashes, with window sills, 7 ft. 10in. by 4 ft.
87 Four pairs of ditto, ditto
88 Four pairs of ditto, ditto
89 Four pairs of ditto, ditto
90 Two pairs of ditto and 2 pairs of half - circular - headed windows, 9 ft. 5in. by 2ft. 9 in. with window sills
91 Four pairs of ditto, 8ft. 3in. by 4 ft.
92 Four pairs of ditto, ditto
93 Four pairs of ditto, ditto
94 Four pairs of ditto, ditto
95 Two pairs of ditto, ditto and 2 half - circular fan lights
96 Four pairs of circular - headed ditto, 9 ft. 6in. by 4ft. 2 in., with window sills
97 Two pairs of mahogany ditto, 7ft. 10in. by 4ft., window sills and 3 fan lights
98 Five pairs of circular - headed oak glazed sashes and window sills, 13ft. 5in. by 6ft. 4in., pair of glazed folding - doors and fanlight
99 Twenty - six sham or blind sashes, 3ft. 2in. by 3ft. 1in. each
100 Quantity of unglazed sashes and quantity of lattice glazed
101 A lot of glazed and unglazed sashes and window sills
102 A lot

Miscellaneous

LOT 103 Quantity of ash poles, from 8ft. to 14ft. long
104 Quantity of ditto
105 Quantity of ditto
106 Quantity of hurdle stakes
107 Quantity of ditto
108 Chaff cutting machine, water cart and pair of harrows
109 Twenty six oak joists and pieces of quarter, about 10ft. long each

Stone and Wood Columns, Pilasters etc.

LOT 110 Four stone fluted Doric columns, 4 pilasters and 2 corner pilasters, with their caps and bases, 10ft. high each
111 Six Doric columns, 9ft. 6in. high each and 2 three - quarter columns
112 Carved freestone frieze, about 44 ft and 4 pilaster bases and capitals

113 Two stone arches and 5 Ionic columns
114 Forty - seven ft. of carved block cornice and 40ft. of moulding
115 An oak fanlight, supported by bold trusses, and sundry oak panelling
116 Three sham doors, 7ft. by 3ft. 4, pair of folding doors, 6ft. 8 by 4ft. 6 and half circular head
117 Four sweep panelled doors, 6ft. 4 by 2ft. 10 each
118 A panelled door, with fluted pilasters and pediment head, extreme size 10ft. by 5ft. 6 and carved door - cap and pair of trusses.
119 Twelve pilasters and 4 corner ditto, the panels of pilaster, the Corinthian capitals, and double bases, elaborately and delicately carved
120 One hundred and twenty - five feet of carved moulding, to correspond with the pilasters
121 A quantity of panelling, window shutters etc. with carved mouldings to correspond
122 A lot of panelling
123 Six Composite fluted pilasters and 4 corner ditto, 10ft. high and 4 others, 8ft. high
124 Eight fluted Composite pilasters and 4 corner ditto, 9ft. 3 high
125 Eight ditto
126 Six fluted Ionic columns, 6ft 6 high
127 Four fluted Corinthian columns, 9ft. high and 2 Composite ditto, 10ft. high
128 Two carved wood chimney - pieces
129 A quantity of panelling, pedestals, mouldings and a pediment
130 A quantity of carved moulding
131 A quantity of ditto
132 Sundry plasters and fixings
133 Ten pair of panelled window - shutters
134 Two doors, quantity of panelling, and wood chimney piece
135 A lot of sundries
136 Six moulded frames, quantity of door stiles and a lot of window - shutters
137 A lot of panelling and a pediment
138 Fifty - nine mahogany balustrades and 60ft. of handrail
139 Two Therm pedestals, piano, billiard - table and sundries
140 A lot of sundries
141 Fifty feet of stone carved moulding
142 A lot of sundries
143 A ditto
144 A lot

Appendix 7

Rooms in Hunstrete House in 1891

The following list of rooms is taken from an inventory compiled in meticulous detail including any broken items!

Best Bedroom
Bedroom Over Dining Room
Bedroom over Mr Popham's Morning Room
Bedroom Left Of Housemaids' Cupboard (Young Ladies' Room)
Bedroom Right Of Housemaids' Cupboard (Governess's Room)
Bedroom To The Right Of Ditto (Housekeeper's Room)
Servants Bedroom Looking To Stable
Bedroom With Half Glass Door Looking To Lawn
Right Bedroom Top Of Kitchen Stairs
Linen Cupboard
Left Bedroom Top Of Kitchen Stairs
Bedroom Landing
Housemaids' Cupboard
Best Staircase With Landing, Entrance Hall And Conservatory
Drawing Room
Dining Room
Morning Room(Formerly Mr Popham's Bedroom)
Gunroom Adjoining (Leading To Stable Yard)
Lamproom Near
Here Are Wine Cellars
Schoolroom
Passage Outside Schoolroom
Butler's Pantry
Housekeeper's Room
China and Glass
Kitchen
Outside Kitchen
Scullery
Larder
Servants' Hall
Knife House
Bedrooms Over Coachhouse And Stable (3)
Dark Room
Harness Room
Coach House
Wood House

Appendix 8

Listed Buildings - as at 13th December 1985

This is a list of buildings deemed to be of special architectural or historic interest by the Secretary of State in consultation with the appropriate specialists in this field.

Hunstrete House Grade 11
House, flanking wall and west wing. Ashlar, rubble, slate hipped roofs. U-plan. Entrance front has 2 storeys, 7 windows all sashes, the much taller ground floor ones are cut through the cill band, off - centre right is a reset mid -C18 doorcase, curved pediment with coat of arms and swags, pilasters moulded round arch, above is a plat band and plain parapet; at left garden elevation has 2 storeys, 9 windows, sashes, first 3 are as main front then parapet sweeps down (for a while there are 2 plat bands), ground floor has cill band. A circa 2m. high rubble wall connects main block to hipped west wing, adjacent main elevation this has 2 storeys, 2 windows, sashes on cill band below, 6-pane sashes above, plat band, parapet, return elevation has 6 windows now altered to paired sashes. Within courtyard made by low C20 wing, main block shows large stairhead tri-partite window, remainder much altered.

***Ice House** - about 120 metres north of Hunstrete House*
Ice house. Mid C19. Rubble, brick, pantile roof. A pointed vault, oblong plan, brick - lined room about 4m by 3m by 5m. high, to the north a 10m. long tunnel about 1.5m wide, rubble walled with flagstone ceiling, there is a plain square opening high in the gable end of the vaulted main room which lets into a small gabled shed with a plain door; all this structure except the shed is covered by a large mound of insulating earth.

***Arcade** - about 200 metres north of Hunstrete House*
Arcade. Fragment of earlier house of c. 1700. Ashlar. An arcade of rusticated masonry, 5 round headed arches, imposts, vouissors, keystones above are fragments of cills. A remnant of the very large house once on this site the doorcase of which is now reset in the nearby Hunstrete House.

***Hunstrete** - nos 10 and 11*
Pair of cottages. Mid C19. Coursed rubble, triple Roman tile roofs with raised copes verges. Picturesque composition. Two storeys, 4 windows, 2 and 3-light multi- pane casements under segmental heads, those to the left in full height gable with quatrefoil, cottage to right has lower central 2 storey gabled porch with 4-centred arch door, 2-light window above, similar window to right, lean-to in window as front and a single light in a gabled eaves dormer; right return elevation has expressed stack. Interior not inspected.

Appendix 9

Inventory of Popham Plate - 1844

The late Edward William Leyborne Popham, by a codicil to his will 1st Nov.1843 decreed that pieces of silver he had collected were to be added to 'The Popham Plate' and form part of that collection. His intention was that subsequent owners of the Popham estates should enjoy them as an heirloom. He directed that a proper inventory be made on his death and a copy deposited with the title deeds of the Popham property for the better information of his heirs.

An extensive list follows and includes:
Three dozen table forks with crest of stag's head
Sixteen ditto with eagle crest
Six ice pails

Much of the plate was sold on 24th November 1891 including the ice pails described as

A Pair of Partly Fluted Ice Pails, with chased handles and gadrooned borders, and fitted with silver liners.
Ditto
Ditto

Sold for a total of £ 1 742 5s 9d by Christie, Mann and Woods.

Appendix 10

Household Inventories

1883
List of heirloom furniture at Littlecote, by rooms.

1890
List of furniture at both properties

1891
Inventory of furniture, china, glass and other effects of Hunstrete House, the property of FWLP - by rooms (compiled from two inventories taken about 1882.)

1892
List of cellar contents of Hunstrete house indicating which to be kept and which to be sold.

List of wines to be forwarded from Hunstrete to Littlecote

Sale of Old and High Class Vintage Wines - property of FLP at the Grand Hotel, Bristol.

1897
List of articles taken from Littlecote to Hunstrete.

1898
List of contents of 6 plate chests and 1 packing case at Lloyd's Bank (London) FWLP. Jewellery, silver etc.

1901
List of linen at Hunstrete House

1905
List of linen from housekeepers cupboard at Hunstrete sent to Mr Popham, 'St Catherines', Sea View, Isle of Wight.

1908
List of bedding from Hunstrete Estate stored by Powell and Powell, Bath. Property of Arthur Treymayne Buller.

Appendix 11

Houndstreet Estate Timber Valuation c. 1775

Manors of: Pensford, Publow and Woollard, Compton Dando, Houndstreet, Chellwood, Farmbury and Marksbury.

Below is given the timber at Houndstreet

In the garden	9 oak trees (1pollard 8 maiden)
In the court	1 oak tree (maiden)
In the park	46 oak trees (13 pollard 33 maiden)
In the common	11 oak trees (all maiden)
In the wood	419
Elsewhere	66
In the common	11 elm trees (all maiden)
In the pound	1 elm tree (maiden)
In the park	87 elm trees (1 pollard 86 maiden)
In ye waste	6 elm trees (maiden)
In ye green	2 elm trees (maiden)
Elsewhere	81
In common wood	18 ash trees (2 pollard 16 maiden)
In the court	3 ash trees
In the park	27 ash trees (2 pollard 25 maiden)
Elsewhere	45 ash trees
In the park	14 witch hazel

Appendix 12

Survey and Valuation of the Manor of Houndstreet with Marksbury etc . . . 1807

As to ornament great part of this Park is so irregular and uneven, that if the intended new Plantations are judiciously made, great effect as to beauty will be produced; and provided Forest Trees have the preference in such Plantations they will in the course of time, carry great profit likewise; but no Plantations can in our opinion be raised, or any beauty affected in the Park to any extent, unless the rabbits be kept very much under, if not totally destroyed, for their burrowing will not only cause greater deformity, but they will ruin all young Plantations that may be made, except they are protected by walls.

And as to profit, we cannot conceive they can produce so much as might be made from the Agistment of Cattle upon an improved Herbage, besides which they must tend to starve the Deer, and all other Cattle that are turned into the Park.

We are sensible we give this advice against a strong bias in favor of the Rabbits, but we cannot bring ourselves to recommend a continuance of the present slovenly state of this large tract of land, by continuing it in Warren - On the contrary, we think it our duty to recommend the keeping of better stock, such as Sheep and Scotch or Welsh Bullocks, which instead of impoverishing the soil, as Rabbits do, will lend greatly to its improvement. Besides which, we think that if eighty acres at the bottom, below the Keeper's House, were taken off, and converted into a Farm according to the Norfolk System of Husbandry, by managing it under a four course shift, in equal quantities of Wheat, Oats, Clover and Turnips, it would be a great object of profit and convenience to the family residing in the Mansion House and a small Barn and Stable erected near the Keeper's House, would be all the additional Buildings that would be required on this occasion.

Appendix 13

Deposition of mother Barnes the Midwife

" Thes are to testefye my knowledge touchinge certeyne speche wch. Mother Barnes of Shefforde uttered not longe before her deathe in the presence of me and others videlt. That there came unto her house at Shefforde, two men in maner leeke servinge men in blacke fryse cotes, rydinge upon very good geldinges or horses wch. declared unto her that theyre mystres (as they then called her) nameing Mrs. Knevett, wch. is now the wyfe of Sr. Henry Knevett, Knighte of Wiltesh. had sente by them comendacions unto her prayenge her of all loves to come unto her forthwt. accordinge to her promise; shee beinge as they said, at that tyme neare her tyme of traveyle of childe whoe presently prepared her selfe redy to ryde, and beinge somwhat late in the eveninge, shee departed from her said house in the company of the two before recited persons, whoe rode wth. her the moste parte of alle that nighte. And towardes daye, they broughte her unto a fayre house and alighted her neere a doore of the said house at the wch. doore one of those that broughte her made some little noyse, eyther by knockinge or ryncinge of some belle, wheruppon there came to the said doore a tall slender gentleman, having uppon hym a longe goune of blacke velvett, and bringinge a lighte wth, him, whoe so soone as shee was entred into the said doore, made faste the same, and shutt out those that broughte her, and presently broughte her upp a stayres into a fayre and a large greate chambre, beinge hanged all aboute wth. arras in the wch. chambre there was a chymney, and therein was a great fyre and from thence through the said chambre shee was conveyed unto an other chambre leeke proprcion, and hanged in leeke sorte as the fyrste was, in the wch. chambre was also a chymney and a greate fyre, and passinge through the said seconde chambre, shee was broughte into a thyrde chambre, hanged also rychlye wth.arras, in the wch. chambre there was a bed rychlye and gorgeouslye furnished the curteynes of the said bed beinge alle close drawen about the said bed. And so soone as shee was entered in at the doore of the laste resited chambre, the said partye in the longe velvet goune ronned softly in her eare sayinge; loe, in yonder bed lyethe the gentle woman that you are sente for to come unto, go unto her and see that yow doe youre uttermost endevoyre towardes her, and yf shee be safely delivered, you shall not fayle of greate rewarde, but if she myscarry in her traveyle, yow shall dye.

Wheruppon, as one amased, she departed from the said gentleman to the beddes syde, fyndinge there a gentlewoman in traveyle, lyenge in greate estate, as by the furniture uppon her and aboute her it dyd appeare, this gentlewoman's face beinge couered eyther wth. a viser or a cell, but wth. wch. I doe not remembre. And shortly after her cominge she was delivered of a man childe, whoe for lacke of other clothes was fayne to be wrayped in the myd - wyfes apron, and so was carreied by the said midwyfe into one of the two fyrste chambres that shee passed throughe at the fyrste wth. the gentleman, fynding the said gentleman there at her coming thither, whoe demaunded of her whether the partye that shee came from was delivered of childe or no, whoe aunswered that shee was safely delivered of a man childe wch. shee there presently shewed him, requiringe him that some provision of clothes might be had to wrapp it wth. alle, who incontinently broughte her to the fyre syde, into the wch. fyre he commaunded her to caste the childe, wheruppon shee kneeled doune unto him, desyringe him that he would not seeke to destroy it, but rather geve it unto her, promisinge him to keep it as her owne, and to be sworne never to diclose it, the wch. thinge the gentleman woulde not yelde unto, but whether by the mydwyfe her selfe, or by him, or by them both I do not perfectly remembere. And so soon as this horrible facte was done, shee was commaunded tp goe backe agayne to the gentlewoman, where she remayned all that day and by nighte was broughte backe agayne by those two men that broughte her thither, whoe sett her some myles distante from her house, but whether two myles or more I doe not remembre. And I demaundinge of her wch. way shee wente in rydinge thither, shee aunswered that as she supposed she wente faste by Dunington Parke, leavinge the saide parke on her righte hande, and demaundinge of her by what houses she traveyled by, shee aunswered that shee traveyled by dyuers houses wch. shee knewe not, and demaundinge ouver or throughe whay waters shee passed, she aunswered shee passed over a greate and a longe bridge wch. as shee tryly supposed was a bridge over the Thames, as by the water wch. passed throughe the said bridge beinge very greate shee dyd imagine.

By me ANTHONYE BRIDGES"

References

Due to the nature of the text the references have not been annotated but are in the order used within the chapter.

All references prefixed SRO are from the Somerset Record Office at Taunton.

The Popham Papers are prefixed with either DD PO or DD Pot.

Those prefixed SRS are publications of the Somerset Record Society.

Chapter 1- Hunstrete House

Sites and Monuments Register for Bath and North East Somerset.
The Saxon Charters and Field Names of Somerset - G. B. Grundy 1935
Bristol and Avon Archaeology - Volume 11 1983. Stantonbury and District in the Tenth Century. M. Costen
The History and Antiquities of the County of Somerset - Volume III. J.Collinson. R. Crutwell 1791
SRS - Volumes 59 and 63. The Glastonbury Chartulary.
SRS - Volume 5. Rentalia et Custumaria.
A West Country Family - Frederick W. Popham. Kemsing (limited edition) 1976
Aubrey's Brief Lives. Edited by Oliver Lawson. Dick, Secker and Warburg 1949
Popham Inventory of 1646 - in private ownership
SRO DD PO 32/2, 32/2a, 32/4 and 32/9 Half Year Accounts 1673 -1707
SRO DD PO 4n Lease of 1702, other leases for same building 1709 and 1731
SRO DD PO 67 Survey of Manors of Houndstreet and Marksbury, with map 1759
SRO DD PO 2j Lease of 1788 referring to lease of 1755
SRO DD PO 104 Statement of Title and Repairs 1831
Article by Michael McGarvie in Somerset and Dorset Notes and Queries. Vol 34 2000
Document re leases of Popham properties 1917 - in private ownership.
SRO DD PO 32 Stewards' Accounts and Vouchers 1649 - 1817
SRO DD PO 42a and 42b Accounts and Vouchers 1782 - 1796
Around Combe Down - Peter Addison. Millstream Books 1998
SRO DD PO 73 Houndstreet Estate - Survey and Valuation, with map, 1806
Journal of a Somerset Rector - John Skinner A.M.Antiquary. Edited by Howard and Peter Coombs. Kingsmead Press 1971
SRO DD PO 34a and 34b Stewards' Accounts 1813 - 1833
Somerset Country Houses and Villages. Truman Press 1909
SRO DD PO 1841 113a Inventories 1844 - 1901

Chapter 2 - Prior Park

The Georgian Buildings of Bath from 1700 - 1830. Walter Eason. Faber and Faber 1969
Prior Park Sale Catalogue 1847
Article in Country Life Magazine. May 18th 1995
Prior Park - J.S. Roche. Burns, Oates and Washbourne Ltd. London 1931
St. Blaise Limited - Archive material

Chapter 3 - Popham Owners of Hunstrete

A West Country Family - Frederick W. Popham. Kemsing (limited edition) 1976
Aubrey's Brief Lives - Edited by Oliver Lawson Dick. Faber and Faber 1948
SRO DD PO 104 Houndstreet Mansion - Statement as to Title and Repairs 1831

Chapter 4 - Water

SRO DD Pot 133 Half Yearly Accounts 1705
SRO DD PO 73 Houndstreet Estate - Survey and Valuation, with map, 1806
Sites and Monuments Register for Bath and North East Somerset.
Bristol and Avon Archaeology - Volume 4 1984. Medieval Fishponds in Somerset. E.Dennison and R.Iles
Journal of a Somerset Rector - John Skinner A.M.Antiquary. Edited by Howard and Peter Coombs. Kingsmead Press 1971
Article in Somerset Guardian June 12th 1894
DD PO 33a Stewards' Accounts 1806
Hunstrete Estate Sale Catalogue 1956

Chapter 5 - Woodland

The History and Antiquities of the County of Somerset - Volume III. J.Collinson. R. Crutwell 1791
SRS - Volumes 59 and 63. The Glastonbury Chartulary.
DD PO 108 Game Preservation and General Estate Management Bonds 1730 - 1802
DD PO 32 Houndstreet Audit 1649 - 1650
SRO DD PO 42a Accounts and Vouchers 1782 - 1796
SRO DD PO 34a Stewards' Accounts 1813 - 1833
SRO DD Pot 133 Half Yearly Accounts 1705
SRO DD PO 67 Survey of Manors of Houndstreet and Marksbury, with map, 1759
SRO DD PO 102 Houndstreet Estate Timber Valuation c.1775
SRO DD Pot 134 Accounts 1770 - 1782
SRO DD PO 32/98 Stewards' Accounts and Vouchers 1649 - 1817
SRO DD PO 33f Stewards' Accounts 1806 - 1812
SRO DD PO 35a and 35f Accounts and Rentals 1813 - 1819
SRO DD PO 78 Houndstreet Estate Survey 1813 - 1815
Hunstrete Estate Sale Catalogue 1956
SRO DD PO 43 Labour and Wages Books 1883 - 1884
Tree Survey - T.P.Marsh 1995

Chapter 6 - The Park

SRO DD Pot 133 Half Yearly Accounts 1705, 1713
SRO DD PO 35a and 35f Accounts and Rentals 1813 - 1819
SRO DD PO 34a Stewards' Accounts 1813 - 1833
T/PH/T1 Tithe Map of Marksbury c.1843
SRO DD PO 32 Stewards' Accounts and Vouchers 1649 - 1817
SRO DD PO 33a Stewards' Accounts 1806 - 1812
SRO DD PO 34a and 34b Stewards' Accounts 1813 - 1833
SRO DD PO 42a and 42b Accounts and Vouchers 1782 - 1796
SRO DD PO 67 Survey of Manors of Houndstreet and Marksbury, with map, 1759
SRO DD PO 73 Houndstreet Estate - Survey and Valuation, with map, 1806
Sites and Monuments Register for Bath and North East Somerset.

Chapter 7 - The Gardens

Article by Dr J Betty in Somerset and Dorset Notes and Queries. Vol 29 1968
Bath Archaeological Trust - Evaluation of Archaeological Implications of the Proposed Enlargement of Lakes at Hunstrete, Avon. Mark Beaton and Marek Lewcum. 1994
SRO DD PO 32/2a, 32/3 and 32/98 Half Year Accounts 1673 -1707
SRO DD PO 4n Lease of 1702, other leases for same building 1709 and 1731
SRO DD PO 67 Survey of Manors of Houndstreet and Marksbury, with map, 1759
The English Country House - Ralph Dutton. Batsford 1949
SRO DD PO 34a Stewards' Accounts 1813 - 1833
SRO DD PO 33a and 33c Stewards' Accounts 1806 - 1812
SRO DD PO 83a Houndstreet Surveys 1828
SRO DD PO 82 Houndstreet and Nyland Estate Maps c. 1825 - 1828
SRO DD PO 42a Carpenter's Accounts and Vouchers 1782 - 1769

Chapter 8- Hunstrete Village

SRO DD PO 67 Survey of Manors of Houndstreet and Marksbury, with map, 1759
SRO T/PH/T1 Tithe Map of Marksbury c.1843
SRO A/AQP 18 Folio 32 Rack's Notes for Marksbury
SRO DD PO 33c Stewards' Accounts 1806 - 1812
SRO DD PO 34a and 34b Stewards' Accounts 1813 - 1833
SRO Census Returns for Marksbury
Hunstrete Estate Sale Catalogue 1956
SRO DD PO 20 Court Papers 1657 - 1795
SRO DD PO 32 Stewards' Accounts and Vouchers 1649 - 1817
SRO DD Pot 129 - 134 Half Yearly Accounts
SRO DD PO 42a and 42b Accounts and Vouchers 1782 - 1796
SRO DD PO 73 Houndstreet Estate - Survey and Valuation, with map, 1806
SRO DD PO 32/2 Stewards' Accounts and Vouchers 1649 - 1817
SRO DD PO 4n Lease of 1702, other leases for same building 1709 and 1731

Chapter 9 - The People of Hunstrete

Somersetshire Pleas (Civil and Criminal) from Rolls of the Itinerant Justices. Edited by E. H. Chadwyn Healey. Somerset Record Society 1897
SRS - Volume 5. Rentalia et Custumaria.
SRO DD PO 57 Abstracts of Leases c. 1740
SRO DD PO 67 Survey of Manors of Houndstreet and Marksbury, with map, 1759
SRO DD PO 4n Lease of 1702, other leases for same building 1709 and 1731
SRO DD Pot 133 Half Yearly Accounts 1705, 1713
SRO DD PO 42 Carpenters etc. Accounts and Vouchers 1782 - 1796
SRO T/PH/T1 Tithe Map of Marksbury 1843
SRO DD PO 59 Register of Leases 1775
SRO T/PH/WAT 1 Terrier of Glastonbury Abbey 1515 - 1516

Chapter 10 - Farming

SRS - Volume 5 Rentalia et Custumaria.
SRO DD PO 73 Houndstreet Estate - Survey and Valuation, with map, 1806
SRO DD PO 67 Survey of Manors of Houndstreet and Marksbury, with map, 1759
SRS - Volumes 59 and 63 The Glastonbury Chartulary.
SRO DD PO 21 Court Rolls 1725 - 1743
SRO DD PO 33c Stewards' Accounts 1806 - 1812
SRO DD PO 32/98 Half Year Accounts 1673 -1707
SRO DD PO 4n Lease of 1702, other leases for same building 1709 and 1731
SRO DD Pot 129 -134 Accounts 1770 - 1782
SRO DD PO 33a, 33d and 33e Stewards' Accounts 1806 - 1812
SRO DD PO 107 Field Books 1822 - 1824
SRO DD PO 43 Labour and Wages Book 1883 - 1884
SRO DD PO 35a, 35c, 35e Accounts and Rentals 1813 - 1819
SRO DD PO 41 Park Book 1820 - 1836
SRO DD PO 42a Carpenters etc. Accounts and Vouchers 1782 - 1796

Chapter 11 - Timber Production

The History and Antiquities of the County of Somerset - Volume III. J.Collinson. R. Crutwell 1791
SRO DD PO 42 Carpenters etc. Accounts and Vouchers 1782 - 1796
SRO DD PO 43 Labour and Wages Book 1883 - 1884
SRO DD PO 33 b and 33f Stewards' Accounts 1806 - 1812

Chapter 12 - Gamekeeping

The Saxon Charters and Field Names of Somerset - G. B. Grundy. 1935
The Wealth and Estates of the Abbey of Glastonbury at the Dissolution in 1539 - Peter Cleary. Curlew Publications 2003
SRO DD PO 108 Game Preservation and General Estate Management Bonds 1730 - 1802
SRO DD PO 43 Labour and Wages Book 1883 - 1884
SRO Census Returns for Marksbury

Chapter 13 - Mining

Popham Inventory of 1646 - in private ownership
SRO DD Pot 133 Stewards' Accounts, 1705, 1713
SRO DD PO 12 Somerset Manors and Parishes - Leases of Minerals 1649 - 1771
SRO DD PO 34a Account Books 1813 - 1833
SRS Volume 97 Coal Mining in Somerset
SRO DD PO 32/2a Half year Accounts 1673 - 1707
SRO DD/RM 22 Leases

Chapter 14 - Law and Order

Somersetshire Pleas (Civil and Criminal) from Rolls of the Itinerant Justices. Edited by E. H. Chadwyn Healey. Somerset Record Society Subscribers 1897
SRO A/AQP 18 Folio 32 Rack's Notes for Marksbury
SRO DD PO 20 Court Papers 1657 - 1795

SRO DD PO 41 Park Books 1820 - 1836
SRO DD PO 108 Game Preservation and General Estate Management Bonds 1730 - 1802
SRO DD PO 34a and 34b Stewards' Accounts 1813 - 1833

Chapter 15 - The Popham Years

Popham Inventory of 1646 - in private ownership
SRO DD PO 32 Household Audit 1649 - 1650
SRO DD PO 32/2 Half year accounts 1649 - 1817
SRO DD PO 4n Lease of 1702
SRO DD PO 32 Stewards' Accounts and Vouchers 1649 - 1817
SRO DD PO 42a and 42b Carpenters etc. Accounts and Vouchers
SRO DD Pot 133 Stewards' Accounts 1705, 1713
SRO DD Pot 144 Accounts 1734 - 1735
SRO DD PO 33a, 33b, 33c, 33d and 33e Stewards' Accounts 1806 - 1812
SRO DD Pot 146 Wine Account 1772 - 1774
SRO DD PO 53 Day Book 1806 -1807
SRO DD PO 35a and 35b Accounts and Rentals 1813 - 1819
SRO DD PO 34b Stewards' Accounts 1813 - 1833
The Diary Of John Harington MP 1646 - 53 Edited by Margaret F. Steig Somerset Record Society 1977
SRO DD PO 67 Survey of Manors of Houndstreet and Marksbury, with map, 1759
SRO DD PO 108 Game Preservation and General Estate Management Bonds 1730 - 1802
SRO T/PH/T1 Tithe Map of Marksbury c.1843
SRO DD Pot 165 Private Correspondence 1707 - 1839

Chapter 16 - Hunstrete at War

The History and Antiquities of the County of Somerset - Volume III. J. Collinson. R. Crutwell 1791
SRS Volume 20 - 1904 Certificate of Musters for Somerset
Somerset in the Civil War and Interregnum - David Underdown. David and Charles 1973
The Civil War in Bath and North Somerset - John Wroughton. Coward and Gerrish 1973
Somerset: The Millennium Book edited by Tom Mayberry and Hilary Binding Somerset Books 1999
Somerset v Hitler - Donald Brown. Countryside Books 1999

Chapter 18 - The American Connection

A West Country Family - Frederick W. Popham. Kemsing (limited edition) 1976
The Popham Family Papers - Bristol Reference Library
Article in American Archaeology Winter 2000 - 2001 Fort St. George - Geoffrey P. Brain

Chapter 19 - Legends

Littlecote - Private Publication 1900
Littlecote Official Guide - P.A.Spreadbury. Photo Precision 1972
The History Of Chelwood - Parsons. Private Publication 1966

Chapter 20 - Archaeological Excavations

Bath Archaeological Trust - Evaluation of Archaeological Implications of the Proposed Enlargement of Lakes at Hunstrete, Avon. Mark Beaton and Marek Lewcun 1994

Bath Archaeological Trust - The Hunstrete House Hotel; A Brief Review of the Documentary Evidence Relating to its History and Development. Mark Beaton and Marek Lewcun 1997

Chapter 21- The Popham Legacy

The New World Tapestry Official Guidebook

Bibliography - General Works of Reference

Aston Michael - Editor - Aspects of the Mediaeval Landscape of Somerset. Somerset County Council 1988

Concise Oxford Dictionary of English Place Names - Eilert Ekwall. Clarendon Press 1960

Down C. G. and Warrington A.J. - History of the Somerset Coalfield. David and Charles 1971

Dunning Robert - Some Somerset Country Houses. Dovecote Press 1991

Gough G.W. - The Mines of Mendip. David and Charles Newton Abbot 1967

Hey David - Editor - The Oxford Companion to Local History. Oxford University Press 1996

Landberg Sylvia - The Medieval Garden. British Museum Press 1995

Littlecote - Private Publication. 1900

Mills A.D. - A Dictionary of English Place Names. Oxford University Press 1991

Penoyre Jane and John - Decorative Plasterwork in the Houses of Somerset 1500 - 1700. Somerset County Council 1994

Pevsner Nikolaus - The Buildings of England: North Somerset and Bristol, Penguin 1958

Richardson John - The Local Historians' Encyclopaedia. Historical Publications 1986

Acknowledgements

I should like to thank the following that gave so freely of their time, knowledge and resources during the research for this book:

The management and staff of Hunstrete House Hotel in particular Richard Gillis
The villagers of Hunstrete and the surrounding area - past and present
Somerset County Record Office - Tom Mayberry and staff
Somerset Studies Library - David Bromwich and staff
Bath Archaeological Trust - Peter Davenport, Mark Beaton and Marek Lewcun
Bob Sides - Bath and North East Somerset archaeologist
Bristol Central Reference Library - staff
Bath Central Reference Library - staff
Wells Library - staff
British Architectural Library
The Royal Institute of British Architects
National Manuscripts Commission
National Monument Archive
English Heritage
Wells Cathedral Archives
Prior Park College
Newton Park College
Bristol Museum and Art Gallery - Sheila Stoddard
St Blaise Construction Limited - Ian Constantinidy
Littlecote House Hotel
Coldharbour Mill
Avon Wildlife Trust
Bathampton Angling Association - Dave Crooks and Graham Biles

Ros Anstey
Eva Baurrova
Dr. Joe Bettey
Barbara Bowes
Jeffrey P. Brain
Patrick Bridges
Lloyd Buck
Barbara Calverley
Peter Cornwell
Steve Crawley
Mr and Mrs J. Dupays
Dr.Pam Gilbey
Tony Gill
Dennis Gilmer
Elizabeth Hawkes
Kate Howe
Maurice Kerby
Barry Lane
Lynne Langan
Sir John Lawson
Elizabeth Lloyd
Brian and Heather Maggs
Michael McGarvie
John Paget
Rebecca Palmer
Mary Payne
Gary Pearce
Edwin Penney
Sally Rey
Douglas Rice
Beatrice Salter
Chris Saunders
R.W.Selwood
Enid Shipp
Gillian Slade
Janet Smith
Ann Stachowski
Madge Treeby
Keith Trussler
Ethel Tucker
John Tucker
Bill Tyley
Tony and Linda Warren
Douglas White
Janee White
Margaret Wilson
Brian Woodham
Doreen Wyatt

Also those who provided encouragement and support during what, at times, felt like an insurmountable and unending task, particularly my family and friends.

Photographs, maps and documents, on the pages indicated, are reproduced by kind permission of the following:

Bath Archaeological Trust 163, 164, 165, 166, 167
The Bees Family 109
Susan Elizabeth Caola 20, 26, 33, 34, 36, 52, 64, 68, 159
Jack and Peggy Carpenter 108, 127
Ed and Susan Cunningham 156, 157
John and Thea Dupays 16, 67
Richard Gillis 32
Robert Hartley 19
Jane Hughes 110
Hunstrete House Hotel 25
Sir John Lawson 46, 49, 102, 176
Littlecote House Hotel 43
Elizabeth Lloyd 20, 29, 38, 48, 54, 55, 56, 76, 77, 78, 108, 113, 114, 117, 120, 122, 124, 125, 138, 139, 142, 143, 153
Mary Meerabux 50, 100
Peter and Stephanie Melhuish 85
Rosemary Murphy 8, 81
John and Phillipa Paget 10
Gary Pearce 62
Jane and Roger Pearce 92
Edwin Penney 144
The Leyborne Popham Family 47, 174
J. R. Ridges 12
Gillian Slade 78
Somerset Archive and Record Service 6, 7, 14, 83, 84, 103, 118, 130, 131, 135, 140, 162
Ann Stachowski 147
St. Blaise Limited 35
The family of Mrs G. Tait 21
Madge Treeby 145
Linda and Tony Warren 123
Tim and Toni Warren 98, 99
Margaret Wilson 41, 174